# Leading the Health Care Revolution

## A Reengineering Mandate

# Leading the Health Care Revolution

## A Reengineering Mandate

GARY D. KISSLER

Management Series

American College of Healthcare Executives

99   98   97   96            5   4   3   2


**Library of Congress Cataloging-in-Publication Data**

Kissler, Gary D.
   Leading the health care revolution : a reengineering mandate / Gary D. Kissler.
      p.      cm.
   Includes bibliographical references and index.
   ISBN 1-56793-036-0 (pbk. : alk. paper)
   1. Health services administration—United States.
2. Reengineering (Management)—United States.   3. Health care reform—United States.   I. Title.
RA395.A3K55      1996      362.1'068—dc20      95-36796 CIP


The paper used in this publication meets the minimum requirements of American National Standard for Information Sciences—Permanence of Paper for Printed Library Materials, ANSI Z39.48-1984.  ∞ ™


Health Administration Press
A division of the Foundation of the
   American College of Healthcare Executives
One North Franklin Street
Chicago, IL 60606
(312) 424-2800

*To my parents, who made me possible,
and to my wife, who demonstrates incredible
forbearance when I am not.*

# Contents

# Preface

**F**EW INDUSTRIES have faced the kind of turmoil found in health care. Those involved often feel as though they have inadvertently stepped inside a "cosmic blender." Yet this turbulence offers a great opportunity for people with insights gained from other industries to team up with health care leaders to find creative ways to improve performance.

For several years I have been working with organizations facing the need for rapid and major change. It has been a rewarding, albeit trying, experience for all. Part of the frustration comes from not knowing what to do. Part comes from knowing what to do but not how to do it. And part comes from underestimating the level of commitment needed to do it. Such commitment takes two forms: organizational and personal.

Many organizations attempt to address the need for change without appreciating how high the "price of admission" will be. They are shocked to find how much time, effort, and resources change requires. On a more personal level, those leading the effort are often unprepared to take on their role. Either they are uncomfortable with the personal exposure, or they lack the courage to pursue change in the face of ambiguity and—of course—resistance from nearly every source imaginable.

Working in the health care industry has underscored for me the need to address these issues. Only the "awareness-impaired" could have missed the national call for a change in our health care system. Yet I continue to be amazed at how long it is taking for this call to be translated into action.

As part of an assignment in a major health care business, I helped identify, design, and develop an approach to reorganization that would be sufficiently robust to help the organization move through the turbulence of reform. This required examining a number of management options to see which could match the needs of the organization. The only approach that seemed close was one that was being called "reengineering" in the management literature. Closely examining the reengineering literature allowed me to appreciate the strengths of the approach and the potential for adapting it to the needs of the health care industry. This book is the result of that multiyear effort, in addition to a reflection on my past experience.

## THE AUDIENCE

From the start, I knew that reengineering would affect a broad base of people at several levels in health care organizations. Specifically, I needed to create a source of information that would be of use to the following:

- Board directors and senior executives
- Vice presidents, directors, and senior managers
- Hospital administrators and chiefs of operations
- Physician managers and directors of nursing
- Vice presidents and directors of product development, claims management, and provider networks
- TQM/CQI representatives and directors of quality assurance and utilization review
- Human resources and information systems professionals and management engineers
- Team members responsible for redesigning business and clinical processes.

These individuals, collectively, are the only ones capable of bringing about the changes required in the health care industry. For them, I have written this book with one purpose in mind: bringing radical change to the entire industry. By bringing health care reengineering to the attention of this group, I hope to do just that.

## CHAPTER OVERVIEW

Mobilizing these groups to action is a tall order, because each of them has slightly different concerns when it comes to the redesign of health care delivery. To address this, I have chosen the following sequence for the book's chapters.

## Chapter 1: Case for Action

This chapter describes the global forces affecting the "customers" of the health care industry and the specific challenges within the industry itself. It reviews issues pertaining to customers, hospitals, insurers, HMOs, pharmaceutical companies, suppliers, physicians, and nurses. The objective is to help the reader appreciate the scope of the challenge and to conclude that the magnitude of the challenge justifies health care reengineering.

## Chapter 2: Reengineering Overview

To provide a base for building a health care reengineering effort, this chapter offers an introduction to key issues in reengineering. It includes definitions, principles, techniques, and models, as well as insights into what an executive team must do to set the stage for reengineering. The executive team must establish an organizational vision, develop a strategy to achieve it, and identify the key capabilities that make the organization stand out in the marketplace. Executive teams also identify and choose core processes and supporting business processes that need to be redesigned. Overall, then, the chapter helps build an understanding of what is—and is not—part of a reengineering effort.

## Chapter 3: A Matter of Choice

The health care industry, like many others, has pursued various approaches to gaining improvements in performance. This chapter compares and contrasts reengineering with five alternatives: quality programs (TQM/CQI), sociotechnical systems, employee involvement, downsizing, and automation. The discussion illustrates that reengineering is preferable to other approaches because of its focus on business processes, its insistence on "creatively destroying" current processes, and its ambitious performance target of 100 percent improvement or better. The chapter helps explain the synergy between reengineering and quality programs, why *both* types of programs are essential, and how one connects to the other. It includes examples of achievements in the areas of cost, quality, and access by several health care organizations that have pursued reengineering efforts.

## Chapter 4: Reengineering the Business through Process Redesign

There are two major parts of health care reengineering. First, one must learn how to "wrap" an organization around the effort—to direct and sustain it, as well as implement its outcomes. This effort is referred to as *business reengineering*, and this chapter defines it, explains its objectives, and provides a model to guide the work required to achieve it.

The second part is the work done by teams of people who are asked to redesign the core processes within a health care organization. This chapter describes the work as *process reengineering* and offers a five-step model for guiding the team's work. It includes information on how the teams are formed and trained.

## Chapter 5: In Search of Processes

A major stumbling block within reengineering is having to identify core processes and supporting business processes. Although the reengineering literature has shed some light on the issue in other industries, it has largely ignored health care. This chapter examines key capabilities, core processes, and business processes, with specific emphasis on those pertaining to health care organizations.

Redesign teams are expected to come up with creative options to meet the performance targets set by senior executives. This can be a very difficult task. To make it somewhat easier, this chapter offers a number of general redesign options that teams outside health care have used, and shows health care examples that fit within each of these options.

## Chapter 6: Price of Admission

Far too many reengineering efforts have failed. The numbers in the management literature range from 25 to 70 percent. The reason for these debacles is not a mystery. This chapter offers examples of the commitment required from an organization that wants to pursue reengineering. It also presents examples of organizations that have failed, and explains why. Suggestions about how to avoid the potential pitfalls of reengineering are offered, along with a checklist to help organizations assess their "reengineering readiness." This chapter offers a candid view of the political commitment required to succeed at health care reengineering.

## Chapter 7: Change Management

There have been some significant misinterpretations of reengineering, including the notion that it focuses on process redesign, and that nothing else is of much consequence. In fact, reengineering is a form of large-scale organization change. A health care organization

pursuing reengineering needs to embed change management principles within its effort. This chapter describes how this is done
and offers specific examples of change management principles,
showing where they fit within the business reengineering model.
Insights are offered to help understand those who lead the effort,
those who resist it, and others caught in the middle.

## Chapter 8: Case Studies in Health Care Reengineering

To help convey a "real life" interpretation of health care reengineering, three case studies are included in this chapter. In each one a
description of the organization and its "case for action" is provided
to help explain why reengineering was chosen. Further description
of the way these organizations set the stage for and applied this
approach is offered. Some "lessons learned" are offered, and the
kinds of performance gains that are being realized or anticipated
in each case are described.

# OTHER MATTERS

In my previous book, *The Change Riders*, I tried to provide
guidance to managers caught up in the turbulence of change.
Since then I have come to have an even greater appreciation of
just how difficult this job is in the health care industry. Few other
industries have found themselves in a more paradoxical situation.
Health care has been buffered from calls for change for so long
that its managers often lack the experience needed to manage the
magnitude of change they face. They were on my mind as I wrote
this book.

## Confessions of a Mutant Cog

One of the more unpleasant revelations many of us discover is that
we work inside machine bureaucracies that insist on being served
before their customers. Those who have the temerity to point this
out find themselves regarded as "mutant cogs" in what others
consider as a well-tuned machine. When good people are pitted
against a bad process, the process wins. I speak from considerable
personal experience.

Reengineering offers significant promise, however, for those
who have felt condemned to spend their lives staring at the
underside of mediocrity. There has never been a more powerful
approach to come along. I am hopeful that kindred "cogs" will join
me in using it to create a better "fit" for ourselves by refocusing
our organizations on market needs as opposed to internal ones.

Anyone who has tried to write about this kind of subject will tell you it is a daunting task. First, reengineering is a fairly abstract subject and therefore requires examples to help bring it to life. Second, one risks creating a "windy" and jargon-laden monologue that creates far too much distance between the author and the reader. I have carried forward the tradition started in my previous book—that is, I have chosen a conversational style because it is a conversation we should be having. So, be prepared for some personal commentary that will stray from the more typical role of "information conduit."

# Acknowledgments

**O**VER THE past few years I have had the privilege of working with people who were committed to bringing reengineering to the health care industry. They come from different types of health care businesses and assume different levels of responsibility. Yet they share one common view: health care needs to undergo dramatic change.

Adapting the general concept of reengineering to the specific needs of an organization is a demanding challenge. A group I worked with was willing to engage in strong (and frequently contentious) debate, guided by deep, personal, intellectual investment and their own work experiences. Michael Broome, Midge Colombo, Carl Corsuti, Susan Devane, Joe Grantham, and John Nunn were the "heart" of a business transformation effort that set the stage for reengineering at Blue Cross Blue Shield of Florida. Others who helped shape the direction of the work and provided me with periodic "reality checks" were Helen Applegate, Vicki Bankhead, and Linda Dedmon.

At a recent meeting of health care consultants, someone offered the view that most hospitals don't feel the need for something as demanding as reengineering. If so, those who step forward to pursue reengineering deserve even more credit than I can offer here.

David Hitt, CEO of Methodist Medical Center, and Michael O'Keefe, CEO, and Jeff Macfarland, COO, of Irving Healthcare System exemplify the kind of leadership required to introduce and support a reengineering effort. Their organizations are also fortunate to have people who fill reengineering roles from "czars" to "champions" to being the "yeast" within their overall efforts. Among them, I am deeply indebted to Mike Phelan, Marie Kellum,

Sharon Peters, Neda MacLean, and Jeff Swain, who shared their knowledge and experiences with me and helped me gain a deeper understanding of the variations in process change that they have made successful. It would be hard to overstate the dedication and talent of this group of health care professionals.

Andrea Goldberg has been extremely generous in offering me her advice and support. Her professional life has been spent in health care and she offered examples to underscore the need for—as well as the resistance to—significant change in this industry. My understanding of many of the issues within hospitals and HMOs was increased significantly because of her input.

The bibliography for this book is mute testimony to the intellectual contribution made by researchers and practitioners. It is humbling to find that no matter how hard one works to understand the health care industry, there is so much more to learn. To continue to do so, I have drawn from their work and sincerely appreciate their willingness to enhance our literature.

I continue to be supported by an array of friends who never pass up an opportunity to point out my excesses and help temper any fantasies I may entertain about being talented. Bill Flock, Warren Wilhelm, Barry Fader, Mel Okamoto, and Curtis Dreese are quite good at this, and they know it.

In my previous book, *The Change Riders*, I offered a somewhat unconventional tip of the hat to truly marginal managers who had helped provide countless examples of how not to manage. Here I would like to acknowledge the benefits gained from having been subjected to so many "dumb" business processes. I suspect there is a causal arrow between the two. In any event, such experience, coupled with knowledge of reengineering, means I will never look at business processes in the same way again.

Finally, there is Jan. After a quarter of a century of finding that I am frequently wrong and seldom in doubt, she is quite willing to engage me in debate. She knows it is like wrestling with a pig in the mud. Sooner or later you come to realize the pig enjoys it. And how!

## CHAPTER 1

# A Case for Action

*We don't have customers, only patients.*

A hospital executive

**W**HAT OFTEN passes for arrogance in the health care industry is really more a reflection of historical protection from change. Although it is often held up as unique, health care does have parallels in other industries, like funeral services and higher education. In these service industries, the "customer" has been regarded as relatively powerless in negotiating. Further, because the services they provide are viewed as a societal benefit, they have received greater legislative support than other industries. Wracked by allegations of fraud and coercion, the funeral industry was forced to alter its business practices. The "baby bust" has forced universities to compete for students and remove excess costs, including professors. The health care industry is next in line.

The change facing the health care industry is deceptive. The reason is that it is often broken into little "bits" (such as changing a pay system, organizational structure, or recruiting criteria)— each of which becomes a target for minimal change. The small skirmishes that are won often mask the larger issue: the interdependencies among these bits sum to an overall inefficiency of the system. We have seen many efforts made over the years to address the bits, and it is understandable that people tend to gravitate to such challenges. They are small, demand less intellectual commitment, and can be overcome with minimal resources. They do not involve major political battles, and they produce tangible (albeit meager) results to demonstrate that *something* has been done.

Again, this is not unique—other industries have taken similar approaches and achieved similar modest results. It was only when each was confronted with (and accepted the need for) a greater magnitude of change that they took more aggressive efforts. Since it is becoming clear that legislative reform will not create a similar force for change in the health care industry in the short term, what will? The following elements are likely candidates:

- Global capitation will result in over 200,000 excess specialists.
- Fifty percent of U.S. hospitals will close within five years.
- The uninsured population will increase to 45 million by the year 2000.
- Cost shifting will result in unacceptably high rates for insurance.

To achieve a dramatic change requires an approach designed specifically to do so. Health care reengineering is the approach of choice, given the circumstances facing the health care industry.

## THE GLOBAL CASE

The world faces dramatic forces of change that the health care industry cannot ignore.[1] Although people argue that the health care industry is a local business and, therefore, need not be concerned with global issues, their perspective is implicitly one of "the enemy of a friend," or "a friend's enemy is mine." On the contrary, the global forces have a real impact on health care customers and their relationship to the industry.

### Refocus on Process Technology

Over the years, we have seen greater emphasis on business outcomes than on their underlying processes. Until a few years ago, "process" was regarded as a typically American concern. But there is a growing worldwide awareness that the ability to modify business outcomes is severely limited unless one is capable of understanding process technology and using this knowledge to change it. The dramatic increase in global competition has escalated the need for radical improvements in business products and services. From an individual, industry, or national perspective, the challenge is to master process technology. As we will see, reengineering acknowledges this challenge and offers guidance on how to master it.

## Revising Economic Theology

The U.S. business perspective is clear: the government should not become involved in investment funding. Even its acknowledged role in research and development is viewed with serious misgivings by many. However, one need only consider the role of the Japanese Ministry of International Trade and Industry within Japan's economy or the role of Deutsche Bank within Germany to understand that the United States is at a significant disadvantage. Europe and Japan believe that government should play a significant role in their economic growth. A recent example of this surfaced when the United States lodged a complaint that Airbus was about to begin producing military aircraft, thus allowing them to compete directly with the U.S. defense industry. The basis for the complaint was that Airbus relies on government subsidies, giving it an unfair trade advantage. Such a competitive imbalance will necessarily require U.S. industries to reduce their costs (including health care) and increase efficiencies under these conditions. Unless our global competitors change their "religion," the Unites States will be forced to revise its own.

## New Source of Competitive Advantage

In years past, access to natural resources was regarded as the key to competitive advantage. Insufficient capital and lagging technology were considered formidable barriers to competition. One by one, these resources have been found to be less critical to gaining (or even sustaining) market position. Japan's automobile industry has demonstrated the relative unimportance of having natural resources within the producing country. Its production capacity has outstripped nations that have access to abundant resources within their own boundaries. As for capital and technology, their accessibility is only surpassed by their mobility—thus increasing the likelihood that any position based primarily on them is quite tenuous. This leaves a final resource that is in relatively scarce supply, difficult to develop within a short period of time, and notoriously immobile: people. Human resources will be the dominant competitive weapon in the twenty-first century.

*Human resources will be the dominant competitive weapon in the twenty-first century.*

## World Capital Market

Developing countries have long considered the International Monetary Fund their sole source of funding for economic growth. Further, bankers in just a few countries have been able to influence exchange rates through their collective action. Recently, we have witnessed a radical change in capital markets. The boundaries between debtor and creditor nations are less distinct, and interventions into currency markets are largely irrelevant in the face of the enormous amount of capital outside the influence of government financial institutions. Once one makes adjustments for default rates, inflation rates, and normal changes in currency exchange rates, the conclusion is clear: a world capital market now offers nearly equal access to potential competitors.

## New Leadership Pipeline

Along with the shift toward placing greater emphasis on business processes, we need to reassess business leadership. It is no secret that the career paths leading to top positions in most U.S. organizations do not include the production side of business. In fact, 34 percent of Fortune 500 CEOs come from marketing and 25 percent come from finance. Only 4 percent come from production. Among all U.S. organizations, only 30 percent of top positions are filled by people with a technical background, compared to 70 percent in Europe and Japan. To lead a company whose future depends on a radical change in *technical* processes requires knowledge and experience gained from exposure to that side of the business. The United States now faces international competitors whose top leaders have far more process experience— a key difference in a world focusing on a fundamental reevaluation of how work is organized and performed.

## Revolution in Reverse

Our list of global forces is by no means exhaustive, but it does provide some insight into issues that will affect all organizations, either directly or indirectly. These forces have been in motion for some time—none is a surprise to those who have been involved in the market transitions occurring over the last 10–15 years. In fact, some have gone so far as to call this "the de-industrial revolution."[2] Figure 1.1 shows some of the key issues in this change.

For many of us, our concept of how businesses should operate is based on a number of principles that emerged from the work of early organizational theorists like Frederick W. Taylor, Henri Fayol, Alfred Sloan, Max Weber, and Mary Parker Follett. Span of control. Unity of command. Bureaucracy as desired form. These and many other concepts make up the organizational paradigm derived from the industrial revolution. Now we find that what was once a source of strength and competitive advantage has become the cause of failure.

**Figure 1.1** Key Results of Global Change

## The De-Industrial Revolution

| From | To |
|------|-----|
| Fragmentation ⟶ | Holism |
| Control ⟶ | Commitment |
| Standardization ⟶ | Customization |
| Rigid Boundaries ⟶ | Loose Boundaries |
| Division of Labor ⟶ | Integration |
| Change is Bad ⟶ | Change is Normal |

### From Fragmentation to Holism

An underlying assumption for most of our business structures is that optimal performance comes from breaking down work into its essential elements and requiring strict adherence to rules and standards for how each element is performed. When markets welcomed mass-produced goods and services, this logic made sense. It brought about relative stability and predictability—but at a high price. It required multiple layers of management to choreograph all the pieces of work. To ensure that nothing interfered with this effort, individuality, creativity, and innovation were systematically removed from the work environment.

Today's markets are the mirror image of earlier times. They reward organizations that are nimble and flexible—qualities only attained by aggregating tasks into meaningful wholes and performing them in a manner adaptive to rapidly changing market demands.

### From Control to Commitment

The classic principles of management were based on the notion that people were a source of variable cost. As such, the most important goal was to ensure that workers did not deviate from prescribed work patterns. Compliance was valued more highly than creativity. As the list of standard operating procedures grew to an enormous size, employees learned that the most effective form of corporate sabotage was to follow them.

The flexibility required of organizations today can only come from a reassessment of the employee's role and value. As people are seen as appreciating assets, the previous command and control environment will have to give way to one that offers them a voice and choice. Greater responsibility will become more tightly linked to increased accountability—and both will be played out more often within teams whose rewards reflect the organizational performance they produce.

## From Standardization to Customization

There never was a "mass market." It was a myth created to explain buying habits under conditions of limited choice. Over the years the business community perpetuated the myth through business school curricula and organizational assignments that fit the model. Production standards, accounting methods, and the entire production pipeline were designed around this concept.

For early pioneers willing to radically redesign their processes and use technology to enable their efforts, the rewards have been substantial. Customers believe that each person can receive a unique product or service on request. For instance, Toyota creates the illusion of unlimited customer choice of options through its rapid response time and wide variety of choices. Regardless of the degree to which the perception of "mass customization" reflects reality, it most certainly threatens the mass market concept. Rising consumer expectations virtually guarantee further movement toward customization.

## From Rigid Boundaries to Loose Boundaries

The hierarchies that made up the classic business structures had distinct boundaries that separated individual, functional, and departmental domains. The logical extension was rigid boundaries between industries and nations.

If reengineering becomes associated with no other major change in thinking, it certainly will be known by its deliberate challenge to fixed boundaries. As we will see later in Chapter 5, realizing the potential for dramatic increases in performance requires rethinking the utility of traditional organizational boundaries. Multidisciplinary work teams. Organizations outsourcing to their suppliers. Integrated health care delivery systems. Regions of one nation forming economic alliances with other nations. These are just a few of the emerging options.

## From Division of Labor to Integration

Fragmentation of processes created specialists who performed within a narrow band of tasks. It was only a matter of time before this ever-narrowing division of labor imploded. Its fate was hastened by organizations coming to grips with the growing likelihood of their own demise if they didn't provide the increased performance demanded by their markets.

This shift in orientation turns specialization on its head. And it is not just a pendulum swing toward generalists. Even those who preach the gospel of multiskilled people are recognizing that there are human limits and that we need to work more toward groups of people integrating their skills. We will see later how "patient-focused care" has attempted to embrace this concept.

## From Change Is Bad to Change Is Normal

Faced with a relatively stable market and moderate employee expectations, organizations in the past sought to create rigid structures—machine bureaucracies. It was a logical, practical, and quite successful approach. These structures were designed to resist change—and they succeeded beyond anyone's expectation. Ironically, the possibility of a changing market was never given serious consideration, so the structure's weakness was disguised by its strength.

The reengineering perspective suggests that flexibility comes from lateral organizational structures that align redesigned processes and redesigned ways of working. All of this adds up to one thing: *adaptability*. The newer organizational structures are designed deliberately to expect and adapt to change, with less disruption than ever before. In short, all future organizations have to be written in pencil.

## Bitten to Death by Ducks

The movement away from the classic principles associated with the industrial revolution did not begin last week. In fact, most of us have been aware for some time that something was up. But, like the old story of the frog and the boiling water, we kept trying to adjust incrementally, without acknowledging that a rather substantial leap was the only way to survive.

Our all too common approach was to try to nibble around the edges of the problem. This allowed various fads and programs to substitute for a serious focus on real issues. A gaggle of "fixes" took small bites out of the organization, creating a hemorrhaging of resources and yielding minor and often short-lived performance changes.[3] Even worse, many of these efforts—Theory Z, managing by wandering around, zero-base budgeting, quality circles, and many, many more—were unrelated to the overall goals of the organization. I must confess one of my favorites was a program that asked employees who faced unemployment to write their names and desired new jobs on a piece of paper and insert them in balloons, which were to be filled with helium and released. It is little wonder that organizational landscapes are littered with debris, leaving the stench of cynicism in the air.

The waste of time, effort, and money can certainly be cited as a major fault of these short-lived approaches. But this misses the real tragedy. Management deficiencies are the wrong target for any approach. What was—and still is—necessary is to radically alter that fundamental core of the business. Peter Drucker says that the assumptions on which organizations have been built and are being run no longer fit reality.[4] Further, among the various approaches to dealing with this problem, only reengineering and outsourcing are designed to do something altogether different from what is done now.

*What was—and still is—necessary is to radically alter that fundamental core of the business.*

## Cruising the Information Cowpath

A business innovation that has offered great promise, yielded great disappointment, and consumed enormous resources is information technology (IT). When Shoshana Zuboff's book, *In The Age of the Smart Machine,* was published in 1988, information technology capital accounted for 42 percent of total business equipment expenditures in the United States.[5] One year later, 75 million people were using computers at work, home, or school. Zuboff's concern was that technology was being applied to inefficient business processes, what some call "paving the cowpath." Subsequent research has substantiated her concerns.

Massachusetts Institute of Technology professor Lester Thurow contends that, at a macroeconomic level, information technology has fallen short of its promise (see Note 1). His research shows that there is no clear evidence that technology has raised productivity or profitability in the United States. Rather, it appears that investment in technology is correlated with lower levels of both. In the United States, the service sector has more than 85 percent of the installed base of information technology—but it has shown the lowest productivity increases of all sectors since 1982. The best that can be said is that there appears to be no relationship between spending for information technology and subsequent business performance. Of course, this has not kept information technology advocates from claiming enormous potential benefits for the health care industry. However, the reengineering perspective, like Zuboff's, is that the linear application of technology winds up extending the life of outmoded concepts.

One of the reasons that actual improvements from technology remain elusive is that the full impact of technology on organizations is often underestimated. Figure 1.2 lists ten organizational areas that are frequently disrupted by the introduction of technology to an organization. Overlooking the many implications of technology results from viewing technology change as a simple affair—akin to bringing home a new toaster. The fact is that technology is not neutral. Our list of issues suggests that we face a major conundrum: technology appears to hold promise, but there is no demonstrated benefit. Instead, we find major internal disruption when technology change occurs.

In Chapter 2, our discussions of the role of technology will make this point: No computers in the world can save a flawed business model. The problem is not the technology itself, but how it is used. Technology should not be the driver of change, but the enabler. It should not be an enemy disguised as a tool, but a real tool for personal and organizational growth.

*No computers in the world can save a flawed business model.*

Having examined several global forces, shifting business models, and an array of pathetic distractions, let us turn our attention more directly toward the U.S. health care industry, its key dimensions, issues, and the challenges faced by its primary players.

**Figure 1.2** Areas Affected by Information Technology in an Organization

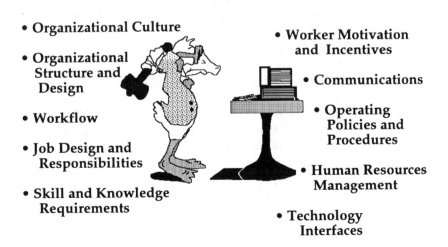

- **Organizational Culture**
- **Organizational Structure and Design**
- **Workflow**
- **Job Design and Responsibilities**
- **Skill and Knowledge Requirements**
- **Worker Motivation and Incentives**
- **Communications**
- **Operating Policies and Procedures**
- **Human Resources Management**
- **Technology Interfaces**

# THE HEALTH CARE CASE

Survival in the health care industry requires acknowledging and accepting the magnitude of change the industry faces. It is said that the most powerful anesthetic is ignorance. Harsh but very often valid. The fact is that few in this industry have a full appreciation for its complexity and interdependencies. Indeed, it is no small accomplishment to gain a working knowledge of any one of its key businesses.

One problem that comes from discussing the health care industry with its various participants is that they feel around the elephant as blind men. Each describes a particular piece as though it were the whole. Yet this is precisely why the interlocking dynamics of this industry so often go unrecognized. Further, it is why people have a knee-jerk aversion to large-scale system change—they underestimate the interdependencies that must be addressed to achieve significant change. Recall the points raised earlier regarding boundaries. Reengineering often requires that we move them. To know how to move boundaries, you need to know where they are and why.

## The Holy Trinity

If there are three "holy" words in health care: they are *cost*, *quality*, and *access*. While they take different forms in different areas of the industry, they are immediately recognizable and interdependent.

- **Cost:** Health care inflation has certainly taken center stage. Its primary drivers are well-known: new technology, research and development costs for drugs, increased longevity leading to a greater volume of care, AIDS, and other ailments requiring a greater intensity of care, malpractice awards, and several others.

- **Quality:** Although currently it receives less immediate attention, quality will be the most dominant issue over time, reflecting both clinical outcomes and the level of service received by customers. The current "cost wars" continue to eclipse the next battlefield—differentiation based on quality. A revolution in metrics—what is being measured—will shape the nature of this confrontation.

- **Access:** Some define the access issue as the number of people uninsured. Others see it in terms of "freedom of choice" to select a particular physician. How our nation chooses to address hidden taxes in the form of cost shifting to cover uninsured people and the increased limits to choice associated with managed care will ultimately frame the role that access plays in the reform debate.

The dramatic changes required in the health care industry will ultimately focus on these key dimensions. Collectively, they serve as a touchstone to anyone who seeks to pursue health care reengineering.

### The Cost Debate

With health care's annual cost of over $900 billion in the United States, approximately 14 percent of our economy, it is easy to understand why increases in cost get attention. Figure 1.3 shows changing rates of health care inflation between 1986 and 1994. The rate of increase in health care costs has actually declined since 1990. There are those who claim this is proof that the marketplace is taking care of the problem without government intervention. Others argue that historically we have seen downturns whenever health care costs became a hot political topic, but that the rate of increase resumed its upward trend once the heat was off. They contend that the *threat* of reform is the key reason for the current improvement.

When one considers government subsidies, population trends, and tax exemptions, it is hard to see how we could stop costs from rising. Managing the *rate* of increase is the challenge.

The power brokers in the industry are physicians, hospitals, and insurers. Only by radically rethinking their organizations and delivery models will the issue of cost be controlled in any meaningful way. Within the context of growing managed care arrangements, the providers must step forward and become more

**Figure 1.3** Changing Rates of Health Care Inflation

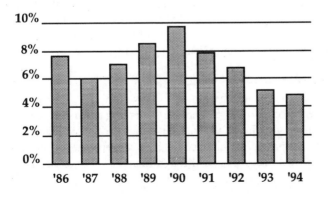

*Source: Bureau of Labor Statistics. Readers should consult B. Belton in the 18 February 1994 USA Today or R. Winslow in the 14 February 1995 Wall Street Journal for more detailed description of these rates.*

heavily involved or face an ever-shrinking degree of autonomy in their delivery of care. We will return to this point later.

Given the intransigence that has so often thwarted meaningful dialogue on this issue, what could change this situation? The answer: global capitation. The major shift in priorities this will bring about can be summed up succinctly: keeping them healthy versus making them well. Coupled with a shift in cost-accounting methods, health care delivery will focus on what can be done to prevent a cost explosion. Preventive care will attain a higher status. We will take more seriously, for example, issues such as the cost of prenatal care versus lifelong support for ailments associated with premature births.

Meanwhile, the corporate customers are not waiting. Their view of health care inflation holds that its major components are price increases, intensity of care, and volume of use. Several methods are currently used to handle the last two components, such as the following:

## Collective Purchasing

It has become clear that employers who band together gain a stronger negotiating position on price by purchasing collectively from providers.

## Quality Methods

Taking a page out of their own total quality management books, employers seek providers who demonstrate the capability to set standards and provide less variation in practice. Employers offer only those health plans shown to be cost-effective.

## Managing Drug Benefits

Watching in horror as their drug plan costs have risen 120 percent over the past ten years, employers are pressuring for change in this area. In addition to negotiating volume discounts, they have encouraged physicians to substitute less costly drugs where appropriate and have pushed for stepped-up utilization reviews to detect patient abuse or dangerous drug interactions.

## Empowering Employees

Actually, this is a combination of "carrot and stick" in terms of encouraging employees to become better consumers of health care and making it financially painful if they do not. Specifically, employees are provided guidance on how to approach providers for care and held accountable through increased deductibles and higher rates of copayment.

## Capitation

More than any other force, employers are the impetus for an ever-growing number of their employees joining health care plans that are based on capitated costs.

## The Uninsured Debate

Part of the debate over access to health care is about how the number of uninsured in the United States—often estimated at 39 million—should actually be established. Some people believe the number overestimates the problem because a large percentage of those counted are actually between jobs for less than a year. Yet, Timothy D. McBride, assistant professor of economics, public policy, and gerontology at the University of Missouri–St. Louis, says his research shows that 56 percent of the uninsured will be uninsured for more than two full years and 77 percent will be uninsured for more than one full year.[6]

Others believe that the 39 million figure should be reduced to include only those who cannot get insurance and not the voluntarily underinsured. Those who support the higher figure contend that the number actually underestimates the problem because it excludes people who are underinsured. They also point out that the uninsured have a higher rate of using acute care— further underscoring the concern that people with insurance are paying for the care of those without coverage.

Regardless of one's position on this debate, one point is inescapable. The number of uninsured people is growing faster than the population. Some people estimate the number will climb to 45 million before the year 2000.[7] All of the cost-cutting throughout the industry will not be able to address this issue. Like it or not, it can only be addressed through the same means that created our uncontrolled cost problem in the first place: government legislation.

## It's the Taxation, Stupid!

Prior to World War II, the linkage between health insurance and employment was practically nonexistent. But the labor shortages during the war, coupled with wage and price controls, put employers in a desperate position. They petitioned Congress to allow them to offer nontaxable health insurance as an enticement to potential employees. Congress agreed to this "temporary" solution and the results met with immediate success.

As expected, Congress attempted to rescind this tax benefit after the war. By this time, employees had come to view such benefits as an entitlement and believed erroneously that the money spent on health premiums was their company's and not their own. The issue was taken up by labor unions who were able to convince Congress to continue the tax treatment of these benefits. As Murphy's Law of Thermodynamics has it: Things get worse under pressure. Thus the seeds were sown for what ultimately came to be an industry with no effective means of controlling cost.[8]

Employers did not question the cost of health plans because with the tax exemption there were no appreciable change in their costs. Physicians were free to pursue treatment regardless of cost. Insurers only served to transfer funds between employers and providers and between employees and themselves. And, of course, users were completely separated from cost. Insured patients wound up buying doctor and hospital services at a deep discount, usually paying less than 20 cents on the dollar out-of-pocket. The predominantly fee-for-service arrangement worked reasonably well for many years, until the explosion in costs of new drugs, advanced technology, increased intensity and volume of care, and other changes brought down the house of cards. Employers were astounded to find their health care costs were outpacing the rate of inflation each year.

Health economists have been writing about the distorting and costly effects of the tax treatment of health benefits for more than 20 years, but politicians have been reluctant even to discuss it. Aside from the primary problem of users separated from cost, the current system also breeds insecurity: People fear losing a benefit that only comes from being employed. Consumers can get a tax break only if their employers buy their health insurance for them, and they are very afraid of the idea of rationing health care.

Polls find that most Americans believe that everyone should be able to obtain needed medical care, but they are at odds over how to reform the financing mechanism for health insurance in a realistic and efficient way. At a minimum, tax reform would need to eliminate the primarily middle-class fear that losing a job means losing health insurance. The employment shift from manufacturing to service jobs is coupled with more part-time employment. The former shift is associated with fewer union-backed health care benefits; the latter with fewer benefits, period. This leaves open the issue of whether or how the government would finance health insurance for those unable to afford it. In short, we find ourselves once again in a familiar corner.

There is no way that cost containment can address the problem of the growing number of uninsured people. Americans face two repugnant options: (1) a hidden tax in the form of cost shifting—

*Customers are taking control of the fate of health care.*

that is, insured people would continue to pick up the tab for the cost of care for the uninsured, or (2) an in-your-face tax that openly acknowledges the need for government financing of health care for the uninsured.

All other options are tied to issues the American people have yet to confront. These include rationing of care, greater sharing of risk through mandated health insurance, and generally allowing the industry to be subject to the market forces found in other industries. What is now deemed unacceptable might very well be embraced if the current system is not brought under control. In the meantime, the best options are those that explore a radical redesign of how care is delivered so as to position current organizations for the continued and unavoidable demand for change.

## The Industry Players

The scope of change in the health care industry is reflected in Figure 1.4—everybody will be affected significantly.[9] This is not a spectator sport. Let us examine each of these players to see the challenges they face.

### Customers

Customers are taking control of the fate of health care. And customers come in many forms, including employers who purchase health care coverage, third party payers, patients, and doctors. It

**Figure 1.4** Key Health Care Industry Players

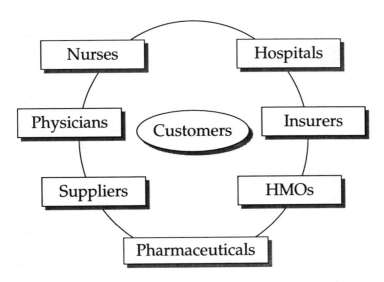

should come as no surprise that their interests do not always coincide—in fact, they are in conflict much of the time.

For patients, this is a particularly stressful time. They are, for the most part, a lost generation, one that had come to view health care as an entitlement provided by their employers. Now, reluctantly, they find themselves held accountable for purchasing health care. Confronting their ignorance over how best to obtain care is painful and they are uncomfortable making decisions about quality and service—issues that they never questioned before costs skyrocketed and they came to fear the loss of care. They are learning to accept as myths that health care is a "right," that someone else should pay for it, and that they should be able to choose any doctor they want. In fact, half of the people whose employers provide health benefits have some restriction on their choice of doctors. This freedom is likely to erode further, fueled by the expansion of managed care to curb costs.

Employers, as discussed earlier, are already taking steps to control their health care costs. Companies like Quaker Oats provide profiles of local hospitals, which include average charges, average length of stay, and how often a particular hospital handles a particular surgery. Medirisk, Inc., a health care consulting firm in Atlanta, offers employers a *Consumer Reports*–like review of local health care, so employers can pass this along to their employees.

United HealthCare Corporation uses analytic tools that examine financial measures, health outcomes, and provider profiles to evaluate and purchase health care. Hospitals are using surveys to assess how satisfied patients are with the services and treatment they receive. For example, St. Barnabas Medical Center in Livingston, New Jersey, uses one such survey developed for the industry by Press, Ganey Associates.

It is worth noting that the government is also a customer in its role as a payer for health care (i.e., Medicare and Medicaid). Recent decisions to reduce the rate of reimbursement for Medicare and Medicaid coverage and proposed movement of elderly on Medicaid into HMOs further underscore the points made about customer pressure for dramatic changes in the delivery of care.

## Hospitals

Pressure to reform health care is certainly hitting hospitals sooner and harder than nearly any of the other industry players. Hospitals represent nearly 40 percent of total health care spending, making them a major target for change. National hospital occupancy is now 62 percent and some predict that this could drop to around 50 percent within the next few years. During this same time frame, flexibility in pricing for hospitals will decrease as health maintenance organizations (HMOs) and preferred provider organizations (PPOs) force hospitals to reduce their prices somewhere between 20 and 40 percent.

These two issues alone are enough to bring most hospitals to their knees. But there is more. The primary source of hospital income has been associated historically with inpatient care. Over the last few years at least 15 percent of inpatient care has moved to outpatient care. Within a few years some believe that half of all care will occur on an outpatient basis.

The most visible reaction of hospitals to all of this pressure has been a growing wave of mergers and alliances. Mergers are often pursued with the intent of gaining efficiency by eliminating duplicate services and maximizing the use of technology. The days of the freestanding hospital appear to be numbered. By 1997 the percentage of hospitals that are part of a multihospital system is expected to grow from 40 to 50 percent.

Profit margins for hospitals today are generally in the 4–5 percent range but price wars, particularly in metropolitan areas, are likely to push these figures to 1–3 percent—perhaps even less. As one might expect, hospitals are responding with severe cost reduction efforts, including the elimination of a large number of middle-management positions. In addition, hospitals are having to rethink how to market their services—with a growing emphasis on building close ties to physicians in the form of physician-hospital organizations (PHOs). Hospitals believe these ties are necessary for them to be able to accept a greater number of fixed-price capitated HMO contracts.

To survive, hospitals will need to redesign how care is delivered and managed. From a reengineering perspective, this will require a radical overhaul of their primary internal administrative and clinical processes and serious consideration of outsourcing noncore activities.

Frankly, the prospects for hospitals are bleak. Together with their historic resistance to change and aversion to risk, many also have insufficient control over their own internal information—a linchpin for focusing any significant redesign efforts. Further, even those who come out winners in the cost game will find themselves facing an even tougher competitive market, one that will require them to differentiate on the basis of outcomes that they have yet to define and quantify.

## Insurers

In a 1994 CBS *"60 Minutes"* broadcast, Senator Sam Nunn stated that large insurers are too big to be disciplined. This is a telling judgment of an industry segment that many believe derives competitive advantage out of creative and complex methods of denying coverage to higher-risk people. In so doing, they have developed a deep and long-term adversarial relationship with patients and providers.

Insurers, for the most part, have waited too long to establish a position within the managed care arena. Traditional indemnity insurance will decelerate from 12 to 7 percent of the insurance market, due largely to customers gaining stronger negotiating positions. Insurers have delayed funding the creation of strong network-based HMOs. As a result, they are losing significant market share to HMOs and to customers who have decided to self-insure.

Their current situation is made all the more precarious because they are unprepared to participate in what they know is the only likely means of survival: integrated health care delivery. When attempting to form integrated systems, they find that they have the following characteristics:

- Have the wrong skills set
- Are slow to act
- Struggle to shift their mindset from assuming risk to managing care.

As if these are not big enough hurdles, they also face a legacy of adversarial relations with the same people they need to seek as partners in order to succeed. In the long run, arrogance has a price.

A close look at their internal operations finds that many insurance companies are bureaucratic, rife with turfism, and staffed by a workforce that has an entitlement perspective that rivals civil service occupations. Top leadership in those that are not-for-profit organizations often has difficulty formulating a new direction. One organization held nine off-site senior executive meetings within a 12-month period to try to gain agreement on the company's direction—and failed. This same organization has been trying to agree on a human resources strategy since 1986.

The first senior executive willing to commit to identifying and pursuing reengineering opportunities in these organizations will wind up feeling like a mosquito in a nudist camp.

## Health Maintenance Organizations

Few would deny that HMOs will continue to become the primary care delivery system in the future. Being the front runner, however, has resulted in their coming under close scrutiny by supporters and critics alike.

Nearly 41 million privately insured people are covered by HMOs, in addition to 3 million Medicaid beneficiaries and over 1 million Medicare beneficiaries. Annual growth in HMO membership ranges between 10 and 20 percent. This growth has clearly captured the attention of HMO competitors.

An HMO is really two businesses. One is insurance; the other health care delivery. And they are under attack on both fronts. Insurers are trying to increase their HMO presence, thus attacking the HMO insurance business. Physician-hospital organizations have the potential for reducing the HMO growth rate by 5–15 percent if they gain greater market presence, thus attacking HMO health care delivery business. In an interesting twist, some PHOs have approached employers with advice on how to self-insure *and* an offer to handle the delivery of health care to employees—thus attacking the HMO on both fronts simultaneously.

The gain in HMO marketshare, however, has come with increased pressure to service this expanded customer base. Among the many challenges HMOs face are the following:

- Increased expenditures for quality assurance, utilization reviews, practice guidelines, and medical outcomes
- Continuing to transform the behavior of doctors toward cost-effective care delivery
- Information systems that are long overdue for being updated and integrated with electronic claims submission
- Needing to work much harder to encourage and monitor preventive care and provide these results to providers and customers.

## Pharmaceuticals

The pharmaceutical industry deserves credit for demonstrating extraordinary political skills. Before health care reform gained its current strength, pharmaceuticals were masterful in currying favor with the medical community, often through gifts, vacation trips, free samples, personal contact, and other incentives.

In the 1980s, while the rest of the economy was in a recession, drug companies and their shareholders averaged more than 15 percent annual growth.[10] During this same period, drug prices increased by two to three times the rate of inflation. All of this helped push them into the spotlight as the debate on reform took shape.

As industry mergers lead to there being only ten global drug companies in the near term, drug customers, represented by large institutional buyers, have reduced the drug companies' pricing flexibility. These pressures are forcing the drug companies to seek ways to further streamline their development and testing processes and causing them to redesign some of their traditional business practices. For example, Merck has begun a telemarketing campaign that has pharmacists contacting doctors to convince them to use one of Merck's drugs. An even more impressive move involves the filling of prescriptions. Merck refers to this effort as replacing the "human dispensing machine" with central warehouse distribution systems. At a time when local pharmacists and hospital pharmacies can fill about 60 prescriptions per hour, Merck's system is capable of filling 10,000 prescriptions in the same amount of time.

Great political finesse was displayed when pharmaceutical companies came under attack by politicians who claimed the companies were making unreasonable profits and charging unfair prices. In marked contrast to the insurance industry's "Harry and Louise" commercials, which attacked various health care reform proposals, the pharmaceuticals quietly lobbied congressional and executive branch members. One legislator described them as "tireless defenders of their own point of view." This view stressed the degree of risk they took in the development and marketing of their products. They also gave open support to such issues as the North American Free Trade Agreement (NAFTA), which gained them favor with legislators. When they did produce television advertisements, the pharmaceutical companies took pains to show how they actually save people money by "discovering" drugs (apparently in tropical rain forests) that prevent having to undergo more expensive surgical procedures.

While protecting themselves on the legislative front, however, the competition among drug companies has continued to intensify. Their internal research and development processes must be streamlined to not only create new drugs, but to do so rapidly and to gain a more rapid evaluation by the U.S. Food and Drug Administration (FDA). Because the outcomes of FDA evaluations are often negative, pharmaceutical companies must be able to redirect resources as soon as possible. This process demands enormous capital expenditure. Further, because investors have come to expect returns of 25 percent or more, any significant deviation in profits would threaten the companies' funding.

## Suppliers

Medical suppliers are encountering a radically changing market. Patient demand for most procedures has been reduced because of increased emphasis on utilization reviews, as well as physicians becoming more conservative. Buyers are considerably more sensitive about price, and suppliers are finding that an increasing number of their products are being moved through distributors. As a result, suppliers are pursuing a zero percent cost growth target—a goal they can only achieve through increased offshore production and by using technology to automate labor-intensive activities. In addition, they are finding that new products are accepted only if they are perceived as cost-effective and they enhance the labor efficiency of physicians.

In addition to lowering their production and overhead costs, suppliers are reducing their sales force. Sales people will no longer have leverage with individual doctors because purchase decisions are being made more often by individuals representing large groups of customers.

## Physicians

The world of autonomous, lone practitioners, whose decisions go largely unchallenged, is fading from sight. Private practices are being purchased at a record rate, and within a couple of years most of the primary care physicians in the country will be aligned with someone.

Despite resisting managed care, physicians are practically climbing over one another to get into provider networks. Others are pushing for legislation that will force networks to accept "any willing provider." This is a particularly thorny issue because the legislation would mandate that, for example, any board-certified physician who agrees to the "rules" of a managed care plan should be allowed to become a member. This would severely affect any effort to base membership on physicians' cost and quality outcomes.

*Despite resisting managed care, physicians are practically climbing over one another to get into provider networks.*

Although a majority of doctors indicate that the U.S. health care system needs fundamental change, they are deeply concerned about the impact of change on how they practice medicine. Already they have seen competition from HMOs drive their billing rates down. Specialists resist the pressure to work as primary care physicians, fearing they will lose their more highly valued competency if they do.

The cost of malpractice insurance is another major issue for physicians. They practice "defensive medicine" (for example, by ordering duplicate tests) to avoid being held liable for medical outcomes beyond their control. However, physicians find it difficult to gain support for tort reform because malpractice awards only constitute 1 percent of the nation's health care bill. Further, some research suggests that a very small number of physicians are responsible for the majority of negligence. A Florida study, for example, found that 3 percent of physicians accounted for 85 percent of all malpractice compensation.[11]

A source of further frustration for doctors is that the lines of authority and accountability are becoming blurred among health care professionals. Doctors are seeing highly trained nurses and other providers encroaching on the domain they regard as reserved for themselves. Any redesign of clinical care that calls for team-based delivery immediately encounters this issue.

As fee-for-service delivery is transformed into what many believe will become global capitation, the impact on specialists will be enormous. Table 1.1 shows one estimate of the resulting surplus of specialists under capitation. Clearly, physicians are at a critical juncture.

Ironically, physicians are in a better position than ever before to influence the future direction of health care delivery. Any effort to redesign practice or clinical management will require their involvement and contribution. In fact, their best chance for retaining an acceptable level of autonomy is to play a leading role in such issues as the development of, and adherence to, practice guidelines. Further, many believe that only physicians are capable of ensuring a sustainable cost-effective environment for health care delivery.

**Table 1.1**
Estimates of Physician Surplus from Global Capitation

| Type of Physician | Total Capitated System Demand | U.S. Supply | Physician Surplus | Physician Shortage |
|---|---|---|---|---|
| Primary care | 124,355 | 209,722 | 85,367 | |
| OB/GYN | 27,026 | 33,697 | 6,671 | |
| General surgery | 13,099 | 38,376 | 25,277 | |
| Orthopedics | 12,325 | 19,138 | 6,813 | |
| Emergency medicine | 12,214 | 14,243 | 2,029 | |
| Anesthesia | 12,435 | 25,981 | 13,546 | |
| Radiology | 15,088 | 8,492 | | 6,596 |
| Psychiatry | 9,451 | 35,163 | 25,712 | |
| Cardiology | 7,074 | 15,862 | 8,788 | |
| Urology | 6,356 | 9,372 | 3,016 | |
| Thoracic surgery | 2,100 | 2,063 | | 37 |
| Neurosurgery | 1,658 | 4,358 | 2,700 | |
| Other specialties | 50,405 | 88,801 | 38,396 | |
| Total | 293,586 | 505,268 | 218,315 | 6,633 |

22

## Nurses

The nursing profession resembles a guild under siege. Nurses are incredulous at how their economic fate has swung like a pendulum over the past few years. In the early 1980s, shortages of trained professionals created opportunities for nurses to gain better-paying positions of greater authority and responsibility. The application of licensing criteria helped ensure that only people with recognized credentials filled these positions. Over time, nurses gained the respect of many physicians whose work was dependent on their competence.

More recently, there have been complaints about the expanding role of nurses in primary care. In particular, the American Medical Association has opposed the role expansion of nurses and is now pitted against the nation's largest nursing professional society, the American Nurses' Association. Nevertheless, nurses are indeed filling these roles, as is evidenced in Missouri, where they can prescribe medication within physician-approved protocols.

Nurses face other conflicts as well. Hospitals seeking performance improvement often choose to replace higher-cost nursing staff with a mix of lower-paid aides to perform routine tasks. In Massachusetts, a survey of 1,800 nurses found that they believe such restructuring puts patients at risk of receiving poor care. The Massachusetts Hospital Association countered that there are no statistics to back up these concerns.

In California, a nurses' union is fighting a hospital reengineering effort because they fear it will lead to layoffs. In fact, many hospitals have found that they could save as much as $25,000 per year for each nurse's job converted to an aide's job. Such efforts would most certainly lead to an oversupply of nurses who would have to get retraining or leave the industry.

Job insecurity has led many nurses and other health professionals to seek the protection of third-party representatives. Hospital workers filed 158 petitions for union elections in 1993, up from only 19 in 1989. Further, unions won 58 percent of health care elections (held to see if there are enough votes for union representation) in 1993—the highest since 1984. Forty-three strikes occurred in 1993, up from 27 in 1992.

In Chapter 7 we will discuss how health care organizations in need of a major shift in direction and a radical redesign of their work processes must turn to effective change management to address such issues. To lose the professional competence of excellent staff by neglecting to change would be a gross error, particularly as our nation's demand for excellent care increases.

## Impact of Mergers and Alignments

The search for more efficient and cost-effective care has led to a desire to integrate pieces of the industry into competitive networks. Current antitrust legislation is being challenged because it inhibits the necessary realignment of industry players. While pursuing legislative relief, several organizations are pushing forward along two other dimensions in their search for alignment opportunities. For example, horizontal mergers are bringing similar businesses together (e.g., Columbia/HCA and HealthTrust). Vertical mergers bring complementary forms of business together (e.g., Blue Cross Blue Shield of Minnesota, Aspen Medical Group).

The potential outcomes of such combinations are viewed with concern by many in the industry.[12] On the one hand, few would deny that routine and common disorders can be treated efficiently by community facilities. However, there is evidence to support the claim that complex care would be delivered more efficiently on a regional basis. The concept of regionalization requires delicate balance. Overconsolidation could result in large and powerful—but less customer-responsive—providers. It might also mean that the development of new procedures and treatments would be limited by pressure to contain experimentation.

Even with a balanced degree of consolidation, the improvements sought for administrative and medical delivery systems will require significant process redesign. Opportunities for synergy will be lost unless those involved recognize that several elements— clinical, contractual, organizational, and behavioral, to name a few—will be affected simultaneously. Without this recognition, there is a greater risk that the organization's logic will run toward simply removing redundancy of services rather than asking if the services should be performed at all. They are more likely to seek to improve current processes rather than gaining dramatic performance improvements through redesign.

## INTEGRATED SERVICE DELIVERY

The health care industry is witnessing a trend that reflects the need to address the interrelated parts of this industry simultaneously.[13] The rapid movement toward a managed care environment requires a new approach to care delivery: the integrated delivery system. Its primary characteristics are the following:

- The ability to offer a full spectrum of care that ranges from preventive care to home health and skilled nursing care

- The capacity to oversee all levels of delivery in terms of cost, quality, and access
- The ability to function with a hybrid of centralization and decentralization within its governing, financial, and operational components.

An integrated delivery system is a classic example of vertical integration. To succeed it needs to overcome an enormous hurdle—horizontal process integration. As we will see in Chapter 2, horizontal integration is a primary objective of reengineering. Horizontal process integration and the financial incentives from capitation keep the integrated delivery service together and make it a formidable force within the changing health care industry. The fundamental base of power in integrated delivery comes from

- The deployment of medical technology and information systems
- Commitment of a skilled and knowledgeable workforce
- Redefined relationships between hospitals and physicians
- Radical redesign of clinical and practice management processes.

The call for integration of health care delivery is certainly not new but the results to date have been marginal at best. Hospitals within such systems, for example, do not appear to gain economies of scale, show greater profitability, provide more charity care, or offer better patient care. This is most likely because these systems were formed as a defensive move against a perceived hostile environment instead of as an attempt to add value in terms of quality of care and patient outcomes. Such outcomes would require these organizations to behave truly as systems instead of loosely federated fiefdoms. One need only examine their current infrastructure (e.g., use of information systems and interunit financial incentives) to conclude that we are witnessing a conflict between contractual integration and operational integration.

## THE MAGNITUDE OF CHANGE

We stand before an industry that is encountering a demand for change that has never occurred before.[14] It has long regarded itself as vitally important to society, but it is dominated by an autonomous power group of physicians that has devalued effective management. The complexity of interaction among its various participants have made the measurement of outcomes so difficult that it sometimes seems that good intentions are rewarded more often than results.

A 1994 *Harvard Business Review* article cited the following barriers that keep the normal rules of competition from operating within the health care industry:

- Payers' incentives make them adversaries of patients and providers.
- Patients' incentives discourage cost sensitivity.
- Fragmented customers have little negotiating power.
- Providers, patients, and payers lack information.
- Providers' incentives increase costs and encourage over-investment.
- Exit barriers protect substandard payers and providers.[15]

*This period of calm is merely chaos taking a rest.*

Unlike past calls for reform, with this one there will be no place to hide. Those who are relieved because of legislative inaction will find that this period of calm is merely chaos taking a rest. The forces for change preceded and will continue beyond the impact of legislation. It is clear that medical and managerial innovation must occur—and quickly.

Under these conditions, top levels of management face two major hurdles. The first is to accurately assess and accept the forces for change. The second is to agree on the magnitude of change their organization must undergo and the time frame within which it must occur. Figure 1.5 shows a matrix that sums up this issue.

For organizations that conclude they need only make minor changes over a relatively long period, normal evolution will generally lead to this end. Others may decide they face a moderate degree of change within a two- to five-year time frame. Under these conditions, most would pursue a continuous improvement approach—indeed, many organizations in the health care industry have made this decision within the last few years.[16]

The current magnitude of change in health care calls for revolutionary thinking at the national, local, and individual level. Most people in the industry recognize we are faced with the prospect of having to make dramatic changes before national redirection at the legislative level. Our discussion of health care reengineering is aimed at this objective.

## SUMMARY

Organizations that choose reengineering as an approach to change do so because they believe they must change dramatically within

**Figure 1.5**  Change Magnitude Matrix

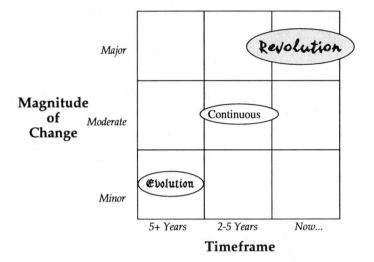

a short period of time. From a global perspective, we see a shift in emphasis toward valuing process technology and aligning the necessary leadership to support it. The role of government in investment funding is being reexamined, and human resources are being acknowledged as the next wave of competitive advantage. These and other forces are resulting in a challenge to management principles that evolved out of the industrial revolution. This legacy, unfortunately, has included fragmented work processes, overemphasis on specialized tasks, deterrence of employee creativity, rigid personal, organizational, and other boundaries, and an inability to cope with changing markets. Organizational responses to these changes have been inadequate, and organizations have lost sight of the need to rethink their fundamental theory of business.

The force for change in health care will come from employers whose health care costs have reached a critical point. Legislative reform will follow, most likely coming first from the states and then from the federal government. Throughout the debate, there are certain issues that refuse to be set aside. One is that the growth in the number of uninsured people will force a change in financing. Another is that legislative decisions have resulted in the current cost control problem and must form the basis for its solution. However, this will only come about after continued and increasing "pain" is experienced by those who think, erroneously, that they are "safe." In fact, all of the major players in the health care industry will either undergo dramatic change or disappear.

These players include customers, hospitals, insurers, HMOs, pharmaceuticals, suppliers, physicians, and nurses. As they all move through this turbulence, many will do so within the context of mergers and alliances that will demand a significant redesign of processes. The emerging organizational form—the integrated delivery system—reflects the need to address horizontal and vertical integration in the managed care environment.

There is little doubt that the magnitude of change within the health care industry requires the use of an approach that can help its players position themselves in the future. Those who choose health care reengineering will have a distinct advantage over those who do not.

## Notes

1. For a detailed review of global forces, see L. Thurow, 1992, *Head on Head* (New York: William Morrow and Company). J. A. Sasseen, R. Neff, S. Hattangadi, and S. Sansoni, 1994, describe the impact of these global forces on how work is performed around the world in their article, "The Winds of Change Blow Everywhere," *Business Week*, (17 October): 92–93.

2. This point of view is articulated by M. Hammer and J. Champy, who provide a thorough review of the issue in their 1993 book, *Reengineering the Corporation* (New York: Harper Business). R. E. Walton, 1985, also discusses the transition described here, in "From Control to Commitment in the Workplace," *Harvard Business Review* 63 (March–April): 77–84.

3. The "quick fix" issue was treated in detail in R. H. Kilmann, 1988, *Beyond the Quick Fix: Managing Five Tracks to Organizational Success* (San Francisco: Jossey-Bass).

4. P. F. Drucker, 1994, provides a useful examination of this issue in "The Theory of the Business," *Harvard Business Review* 72 (September–October): 95–104.

5. S. Zuboff, 1988, also offers an unusually thorough review of the history of management and how information technology has affected it in *In the Age of the Smart Machine* (New York: Basic Books).

6. McBride's letter to *The Wall Street Journal* was printed on 9 February in response to an article by I. M. Stelzer, 1994, "There Is No Health Care Crisis," *The Wall Street Journal*, 25 January.

7. See the reference to the Employee Benefits Research Institute in G. Anders and H. Stout, 1994, "With Congress Stalled, Health Care Is Shaped by the Private Sector," *The Wall Street Journal*, 26 August.

8. Two articles that offer insight here are M. Friedman, 1993, "The Folly of Buying Health Care at the Company Store," *The Wall Street Journal*, 3 February; and G. M. Arnett, 1994, "It's Taxation, Stupid," *The Wall Street Journal*, 29 March.

9. Two sources that offer detailed coverage of issues facing the health care industry are P. Boland, ed., 1993, *Making Managed Healthcare Work* (Gaithersburg, MD: Aspen Publishers); and P. R. Kongstvedt, 1993, *The Managed Health Care Handbook* (Gaithersburg, MD: Aspen Publishers). In addition, I have drawn extensively from K. S. Abramowitz, 1993, "The Future of Healthcare Delivery in America," (New York: Sanford C. Bernstein Company, R. Winslow and G. Anders, 1993, "Medical Industry Scrambles to Keep Up with Changes," *The Wall Street Journal,* 13 September; and L. F. Wolper, 1995, ed., *Health Care Administration,* 2d ed. (Gaithersburg, MD: Aspen Publishers).

10. For example, see M. Waldholz, 1993, "Drug Maker's Image Ills Are Self-Induced," *The Wall Street Journal,* 30 March.

11. R. B. Conlin, 1993, "Are Malpractice Awards the Demon of Health Care?" *USA Today,* 5 May.

12. For example, J. Greene, 1995, "Merger Monopolies," *Modern Healthcare,* 5 December, 38–48, cites research showing that most hospitals find it difficult to achieve efficiencies from eliminating redundancies because of political resistance. There is evidence that charges for ancillary services may actually rise above national levels after a merger. This causes employers to consider managed care alternatives that would force additional competition into the merged hospitals' health care market. For a recent example of a successful restructuring effort by Community Hospitals of Central California, see L. Kertesz's 1995 article, "California System Sees Results from Radical Restructuring," *Modern Healthcare* (24 April): 32–33.

13. In K. Shriver, 1994, "Study: Most Hospitals Will Try Integration Despite Obstacles," *Modern Healthcare,* 14 December, 4, the author points out that 80 percent of 1,191 hospitals surveyed by Deloitte & Touche indicated they would not operate as stand-alone organizations within five years. I am indebted to a body of excellent work describing the gap between the promise and performance of integrated delivery systems. Here I have drawn on an excellent article by S. M. Shortell, 1988, "The Evolution of Hospital Systems: Unfulfilled Promises and Self-Fulfilling Prophecies," *Medical Care Review* 45(20): 177–214 and S. M. Shortell, E. M. Morrison, and B. Friedman, 1992, *Strategic Choices for America's Hospitals* (San Franciso: Jossey-Bass Publishers).

14. Two particularly insightful sources regarding the shift in power that is occurring generally and in health care are A. Toffler, 1990, *PowerShift* (New York: Bantam Books); and R. W. Boss, 1989, *Organization Development in Health Care* (Reading, MA: Addison-Wesley).

15. See E. O. Teisberg, M. E. Porter, and G. B. Brown, 1994, "Making Competition in Health Care Work," *Harvard Business Review* 72 (July–August): 131–41, for significant insights in this area.

16. There remains considerable debate and confusion over where to draw the line between continuous improvement and a more radical shift in performance. In R. K. Reger, J. V. Mullane, L. T. Gustafson, and S. M. DeMarie, 1994, "Creating Earthquakes to Change

Organizational Mindsets," *The Academy of Mangement Executive* 8 (November): 31–47, the authors argue that organizations cannot change rapidly without damaging their sense of identity. The authors seem to misunderstand some of the distinctions between continuous improvement and reengineering (e.g., attributing both with calling for a "blank page approach") and also seem to believe that the *implementation* of reengineering happens all at once. Neither position has appreciable support in the reengineering literature and I am aware of no organizations that have followed this approach in their reengineering efforts. In Chapter 7 a discussion of the path to gaining acceptance of reengineering-related change is offered.

CHAPTER $2$

# Reengineering Overview

*Destroying the organization to save the business. . . .*

Michael Hammer

**E**ARLY PIONEERS in reengineering found that reengineering was a lot like the blind dates arranged for you by your mother. Full of promise; predictable results. Some have even gone so far as to compare it to teenage sex:

- Everyone thinks everyone is doing it.
- Almost no one is really doing it.
- The few who are, are doing it poorly.
- Many brag about successes; few have any.

Yet, American companies will spend billions on business reengineering, and nearly two-thirds of them will fail.[1] Such extraordinary circumstances call for a better understanding of the reengineering approach, particularly among those in the health care industry who are relative newcomers to the approach and who need to improve their odds of succeeding.

## WHAT IT IS

It is helpful to begin with a definition. An early advocate of this approach described reengineering as *"the fundamental rethinking and radical redesign of business processes to achieve dramatic improvement in critical contemporary measures of performance, such as cost, quality, service, and speed."*[2]

Reengineering does not try to fix anything—it openly advocates starting from scratch.

An example will help to illustrate what this might look like in real life. A bank, faced with criticism of its customer service, sent all its tellers to a course on how to treat people in a more friendly and efficient manner. Continuing complaints led to a decision to keep branches open on Saturday mornings. The result in each case was a modest increase in customer satisfaction. What was wrong? The fundamental problem was that the bank's underlying assumptions were not being challenged. The assumptions were these:

- Customers need to do banking by dealing with a human being.
- Banking can only be done when the bank is open.
- The current service process is acceptable; there just is not enough of it.

Of course, we now know the preferred solution: automated teller machines (ATMs). Figure 2.1 shows the improvements that resulted from each of the bank's solutions. The ATM option exemplifies the following key concepts in our definition of reengineering:

- **Radical:** The bank had never done business in this manner before.
- **Dramatic:** The bank actually changed its overall relationship with its customers, leading to unprecedented satisfaction.
- **Process:** The bank did not need to improve its service process; it needed a different one.

It is also worth noting the role of information technology in this example. The bank did not have a bunch of ATMs stored away, hoping to put them to use. Rather, they were aware of the technical capabilities becoming available and used them to enable a radical shift in their customer service process. In short, technology was used as an *enabler* of change—not a driver.

From this example, we can begin to understand the essence of reengineering: creative destruction. Reengineering does not try to *fix* anything—it openly advocates starting from scratch.

## WHAT IT ISN'T

A short time ago, a consulting firm attempted to determine what kinds of things organizations were doing under the banner of "reengineering."[3] Figure 2.2 shows the results. Fewer than half of the respondents, chief executive officers, described reengineering as involving process redesign. In fact, the majority described reengineering as either technological change, product improvement, efficiency improvement, or customer satisfaction. It is worth noting that 9 percent didn't know what they were doing. This sheds some light on why there is such a high failure rate reported for so-called reengineering efforts. If you call something else reengineering— and fail at it—is reengineering at fault?

This poses a dilemma. Although businesses are committing significant resources toward reengineering, their track record is

**Figure 2.1**   Bank Solutions to Increase Customer Satisfaction

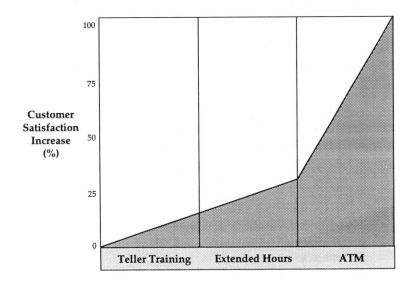

**Figure 2.2**   CEO Definitions of Reengineering

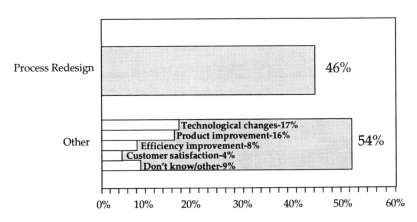

*Reprinted with permission from Gateway Consulting, New York City. © 1993.*

abysmal. We will explore the reasons for this later. But to avoid this failure requires knowing where to start.

## WHERE TO START

To appreciate the nature and potential of reengineering, it is important to understand that it is a form of large-scale organization change. Too often the problems businesses face appear daunting because they are perceived as too complex. To succeed at organizational change requires stripping away artificial complexity and focusing on key areas to manage.

Over a quarter of a century of management research into organizational change indicates that only a few variables determine success or failure.[4] Researchers have chosen a variety of labels for the organizational dimensions they found were critical to manage, but their definitions are remarkably similar. The organizational change model in Figure 2.3 displays these key dimensions.

The model begins with an outer ring of forces that are pushing in on the organization. These environmental forces on a health care business can take various forms: physical (e.g., capacity), regulatory (insurance commissions), or competitive (new entrants gaining market share). As these forces increase, organizations respond by trying to understand them and deciding on how to address them. This often leads to discussions of the desired future direction for the organization (e.g., vision) and a strategy to help realize it. Desired future performance levels are determined at this stage. However, the nemesis to all this planning takes the shape of four key dimensions within the center of the model (leadership,

**Figure 2.3** Organizational Change Model

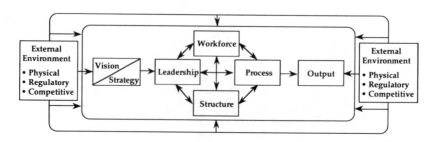

*Source:* The Change Riders: Managing the Power of Change (pp. 127 and 259), © 1991 by G. D. Kissler. Reprinted by permission of Addison-Wesley Publishing Company, Reading, MA.

workforce, structure, and process). For our purposes, each can be defined as follows:

- **Leadership:** Characteristics of management and systems that propel the organization into the future, including vision, power, style, and risk taking
- **Workforce:** Characteristics of the organization's people, including values, skills, knowledge, and motivation
- **Structure:** Roles and relationships among organizational units and individuals
- **Process:** How work is planned, performed, measured, and controlled.

These four dimensions make or break most organizational change efforts. Note that process—a critical element in our reengineering definition—is but one of these dimensions. As we move forward in our overview, we should keep this notion in mind because we will find that successful reengineering efforts—in fact, any large-scale organization change effort—must address all of these dimensions simultaneously.

## A HISTORY LESSON

Reengineering stands on the shoulders of giants. As Figure 2.4 indicates, the components of reengineering have a long history that traces back to process design and F. W. Taylor's scientific study of work at the turn of the century.[5] His approach, scientific management, had as its basic tenet the idea that, through careful analysis, work could be broken down into essential elements. Moreover, by forcing strict adherence to a prescribed set of efficient steps, productivity could be increased. In Taylor's work, we can recognize three distinguishable areas in the study of business that today combine to give reengineering its power: industrial engineering, organizational and behavioral theory, and information and measurement systems.

### Industrial Engineering

The influence of scientific management on industrial engineering in the 1940s can be seen largely in the quantitative approaches carried forward and enhanced after Taylor's work. A subset of this "tool kit" was the analysis of work flow and the identification of problem areas. The "technical" side of sociotechnical systems (STS) refers to the adoption and use of tools based on this approach. By the 1950s, the next wave of development in this area was quality control, which used statistical analysis and sampling techniques to

**Figure 2.4**   The History of Reengineering

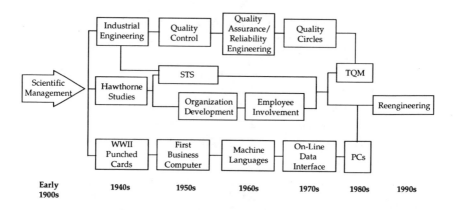

help identify and correct process problems. Quality control developed into a more sophisticated field, quality assurance/reliability engineering, during the 1960s. It gained significant visibility in the U.S. space program.

The 1970s brought to our attention an approach called quality circles, which introduced the use of various techniques (e.g., Pareto charts, fishbone diagrams, and statistical analysis) to groups of people who had direct control over work performance. The modest results from quality circles were attributed to management intransigence about the value of production over quality. During the 1980s it became clear that companies that pursued improved quality were gaining a significant competitive advantage. The loss of market share of U.S. auto makers to their Japanese counterparts confirmed this. Total quality management (TQM) emerged during this time as an approach that focused on meeting customer needs and sought to reduce work process variation to improve quality.

## Organizational and Behavioral Theory

Taylor's work predated much of the early behavioral science research done in the 1940s in military and industrial settings (e.g., Elton Mayo's Hawthorne Studies). This perspective focused on addressing the social needs of the workforce. It led to the emergence of small-group research in the 1950s and the area of behavioral science known as organizational development. The principles of group dynamics, as played out in work settings, formed the basis of the "socio" side of sociotechnical systems, which evolved from focusing on industrial settings to addressing service industries as well. The next stage came during the turbulent 1960s, a time when individuals sought greater control over their lives—including their work lives. Employee involvement took many forms, but the common thread was a deliberate effort to seek the input of employees to gain performance improvement and to allow them to influence the organization's direction. One of the more important insights from this time was that changing the way people work required a realignment of the organization's infrastructure as well. TQM has embraced many of the tenets that emerged from organizational and behavioral theory.

## Information and Measurement Systems

One of the earliest problems facing F. W. Taylor was the management of the data required to measure work efficiency within industrial settings. International Business Machines (IBM) began as a producer of calculators at the time that scientific management was in vogue. From punching buttons on simple calculators, the next major breakthrough was the use of the punched card. This device, first used much earlier to guide weaving looms, was adopted by the U.S. Navy to keep track of individual draftees in the 1940s. Tabulating machines "read" the holes in each card that represented data pertaining to each draftee.

Rudimentary shifts in the use of this technology led to the installation of computers in businesses in the early 1950s. They were used mostly for performing financial tasks. People had to master binary machine logic to use them, and even reading the instructions often required the skills of an electrical engineer. By the 1960s, broader applications of information processing resulted from the development of "languages" that could be learned by a greater number of users. Still, the use of punched cards prevailed until the 1970s, when the interface changed to include on-line screens and keyboards to allow direct manipulation of data. This led to remote computer access through "dumb" terminals that moved the technology closer and closer to the business activity. The 1980s ushered in personal computers and yet another major shift in the interface. The user became the owner, and icons, touch screens, and the mouse dramatically changed the relationship between people and computers.

A virtual explosion of software applications soon spanned all business functions. The critical shift was in the relationship between the computer and the work being performed. Instead of being viewed as a "powerful two-year old" that made labor-intensive things go faster, the computer became a tool to enable the fundamental shift in how work is performed. People began using this technology to challenge assumptions behind management paradigms.

*Perhaps the history of reengineering is best summed up in the old saying, "Never steal a bad idea."*

Finally, in the 1990s, an innovative combination of the techniques, principles, and insights from these three strands has resulted in an approach called "reengineering," perhaps the history of reengineering is best summed up in the old saying, "Never steal a bad idea."

## THE HORIZONTAL REVOLUTION

As Chapter 1 pointed out, there is a global shift toward emphasizing process technology. More specifically, there is a growing recognition that meeting customer requirements means having to orchestrate and integrate processes that cross organizational boundaries. "Managing the white space,"[6] as some people call this process, poses two problems. First, people in functional areas are notoriously poor at communicating and cooperating with one another. Second, it is rare to find anyone who has the responsibility or authority to make them do otherwise.

The standard organizational chart reflects the historic paradigm that organizations should be divided into functional areas. A hospital is expected to have distinct departments such as clinical services, medical affairs, nursing, and so on. Other businesses may be divided into manufacturing, sales, engineering, and so forth. These vertical structures were designed to ensure that there was a sensible career path for specialists and to gain control over the quality of work performed in any given area.

The inadequacy of this organizational model becomes apparent when a customer approaches the business and makes a request. If one were to draw a diagram showing these functions and then trace the path of activities required to meet the customer's request, one would discover a pattern of functional *interrelationships* each time. This path, within reengineering, is called a "core process."

*Make no mistake about it, this is a deliberate effort to decentralize general management decisions.*

In fact, reengineering holds that the key to process redesign is to first identify a core process—or a facsimile thereof—and then to move aggressively to redesign it, to forge an organizational level of performance that creates a sustainable competitive advantage. Companies that take this approach find that it is impossible to gain maximum benefits from process redesign without also changing the culture of the business—that is, its leadership, workforce, structure, and other processes.

This call for a horizontal focus in how organizations *actually* work reflects reengineering's claim that the fragmentation and specialization we described earlier lies at the heart of organizational inefficiency. A lateral organizational structure helps gain flexible advantage in three ways:

- It generates speed.

- It helps sharpen the organization's focus.

- It promotes learning and change.[7]

Make no mistake about it, this is a deliberate effort to decentralize general management decisions. Each core process will require a "mini-general manager" to oversee the lateral coordination. This accountability, as we have pointed out, rarely exists before a reengineering effort is implemented.

## EXECUTIVE STEPS TO REENGINEERING

Reengineering is born and dies in the executive suite. One of the primary reasons so many past efforts at change have failed is that they were not endorsed and driven by top management, so they lacked any meaningful connection to the strategic purpose and direction of the organization. One should expect that a health care reengineering effort that is pursued in a similar manner will fail. It is for this reason that we offer some guidance on the steps that senior management should take before committing their organization to this approach.

Figure 2.5 provides an image of an "executive staircase" that serves as a visual representation of the responsibilities of the senior team with regard to setting the stage for reengineering. They are asked to establish a vision, agree on a strategy, determine desired key capabilities, and then choose the core processes and related business processes that need to be redesigned. Let us examine each of these steps.

**Figure 2.5** The Executive Staircase

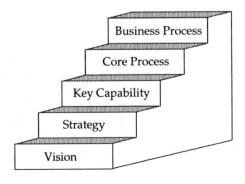

## Vision

*A picture of what an organization wants to become, used as a guiding light for managers, employees, and other stakeholders in bringing about change.*

It was not very many years ago that you got a very odd look if you used the word "vision" in a business setting. One executive expressed his disgust by saying, "I hate the word 'vision' because it implies we don't have one. We do—it is 14 percent return on sales."

Fortunately, more enlightened views have emerged, and creating a future view of a business has become a more widely accepted and pursued goal for better-run and, not incidentally, more profitable businesses.[8] Our definition implies that such an effort refocuses the organization's resources on strategic objectives and winds up stimulating new behavior. Setting the stage for reengineering begins with clearly linking reengineering to the organization's strategy.

As with so many abstract ideas in business, this one has been subject to numerous interpretations, ranging from the mechanical to the ethereal. Reengineering needs to be seen as a means to an end that can be understood and appreciated by the organization. A future view that is developed and articulated clearly by senior management accomplishes this.

Many people mistakenly regard the development of a vision as tantamount to some sort of psychic revelation—an experience to be explained in hushed tones as one might explain a religious conversion. On the contrary, creating a future vision is very hard work. Its purpose can be compared to the two types of drawings used by architects with their clients: blueprints and artists' renderings.

The blueprint helps the buyer understand the physical dimensions, overall design, proportions, and placement of infrastructure. A vision needs to help the organization come to understand the rational side of the change—assuring people that it's achievable. The artist's rendering addresses the buyer's need for an emotional pull. It emphasizes the colors, decoration, and the overall aesthetic desirability of the structure. Similarly, a vision needs to create an emotional pull. Having been shown the map to the future, people now need to be convinced it will be worth the trip.

Too often, however, such exercises result in a sort of bumper sticker slogan, and the impact is lost on any but those who created it. To avoid this, several criteria can be applied to vision statements. A useful vision statement should do the following:

- Suggest competitive positioning.
- Specify what will be different.
- Identify core skills required.
- Provide direction and decision-making guidelines.
- Reveal energizing and enabling shared values.
- Present the rationale for major changes.
- Highlight change leadership themes and symbols.

The new CEO of IBM, Lou Gerstner, was recently quoted as saying that "the last thing IBM needs right now is a vision." Fortunately, the IBM "spin doctors" have come out with an explanation of what Gerstner *really* meant. It seems that he just wanted to avoid simplistic phrases and that he intends to come up with an explicit vision sometime in the—uh—future. The reality all organizations face is that major change without a reasonable view of one's future state results in unfocused effort and a waste of resources.

## Strategy

*Products and services to offer, customers and markets to serve, competitive advantages, product and market priorities, and systems and structures to get there.*

The second step to be taken by senior management in setting the stage for reengineering involves establishing a strategy that will support their vision. Just as reengineering's history helps explain its current popularity, the creation of a strategy has an equally interesting past. In fact, several waves of strategy innovations have occurred over the past 40 years.[9]

One of the innovations that surfaced in the mid-1960s was "experience curves." The theory was that the costs of complex products and services, when corrected for effects of inflation and arbitrary accounting standards, typically decline about 20 to 30 percent with each doubling of experience. By the 1970s, a new trend toward "portfolio management" emerged in the shape of businesses grouped under such labels as dogs (underperforming businesses), stars (profitable, growing businesses), cash cows (profitable, not very fast-growing business), and question marks (not sure what the business is doing). In the late 1970s there was a wave of interest in the "strategic use of debt" to fund investments in diverse enterprises. The accumulation of debt created financial vulnerability and was later exploited by corporate raiders.

The next wave occurred during the early 1980s and focused on "de-averaging of costs" so as to uncover hidden costs that historically had been averaged and allocated. The so-called corporate raiders were largely responsible for the next innovation: "restructuring for advantage." The corporate raiders were people who got financing (generally through junk bonds) that allowed them to buy up a controlling interest of a business, break the organization up, and sell the pieces for a profit. Disposal of unsuccessful businesses, delayering of management, and matching of cash generation with debt service occurred to "lean out" the business portfolio.

The most recent strategic innovation, "time-based competition," has a natural linkage to reengineering. Put simply, when customers are waiting for a value they have decided they want, providing it to them sooner becomes a form of strategic advantage. Reengineering is used to accomplish a radical change in an organization's response time through a radical redesign of its internal business processes.

The challenge, regardless of the strategic direction chosen, is for senior managers to tie reengineering directly to strategic planning.[10] To do so, some have followed these steps:

1. Generate broad scenarios or possible futures that they may encounter.
2. Conduct a competitive analysis of the industry and its strategic segments.
3. Analyze the company's and the competition's core capabilities.
4. Develop a strategic vision and identify strategic options.

The primary goal is to select key capabilities that would allow the organization to pursue multiple strategies to address several possible future challenges in the market. The idea of competing through these key capabilities has emerged as a critical link to subsequent reengineering efforts.

## Key Capability

*The strategic alignment and focus of an organization's core processes to create a competitive advantage by delivering measurable value to the customer.*

The majority of strategies have failed because of poor implementation, not because of a lack of a clear and viable vision. The failure to implement can often be traced back to an inadequate understanding of how to use the organization's capabilities to meet future goals. Thus, the third step toward introducing reengineering asks the senior management team to select those organizational capabilities that are most likely to achieve a competitive advantage.

A somewhat academic debate has developed over the relative importance of an organization's competency versus its capability.[11] A competency has been defined as "the collective learning in the organization, especially the capacity to coordinate diverse production skills and integrate streams of technology." Those who favor focusing on capabilities agree that competency is important but that competencies are not *seen* by customers. A capability, they maintain, is the logical extension of competency such that customers can identify an outcome with measurable and appreciable value. In health care, one might develop a competence in utilization review but never see a patient. To be regarded as a capability, one would need to apply this competency in the actual context of delivering and managing care. So a corporate benefits manager who receives and values the results of utilization reviews experiences a demonstration of capability on the part of those who deliver care to patients. We will stand by our definition of *key capability* and leave the debate for others.

*Senior management must make a deliberate effort to use reengineering as the link between strategy and operations.*

Executives pursuing a capabilities-based strategy adhere to these basic principles:

1. Strategy will be built on business processes, not products and markets.
2. Sustained competitive advantage requires linking a company's core processes to key capabilities that provide superior value to the customer.
3. Key capabilities are created through strategic investments in support infrastructure that links and yet transcends traditional functions.
4. Because key capabilities necessarily cross functions, the champion of a capabilities-based strategy must be the most senior level of management.

The primary advantages that come to organizations that have begun to use their capabilities as a competitive advantage are speed, consistency, agility, acuity, and innovation. However, to gain these advantages, senior management must make a deliberate effort to use reengineering as the link between strategy and operations— thereby "managing the gray zone."

The executive group must agree on how to identify and define key capabilities. Among several criteria that serve as a guide in identifying capabilities are these:

- Capabilities evolve slowly through collective learning and information sharing.

- Their development cannot be speeded up by doubling investment.
- They cannot easily be imitated or acquired by other organizations.
- They convey the image of competitive advantage to customers.
- They achieve synergy in combination with other capabilities.

Looking at businesses in general, we find some excellent examples of key capabilities, including:

- Low-cost position in products or service
- Professional image (quality and reliability)
- User-friendliness in product or service development
- Compatibile or integrative product or service line
- Use of new and innovative technology
- Availability of software and peripherals
- Access to distribution channels
- Highly knowledgeable sales force.

Within the health care industry, key capabilities will fall within the three dimensions we discussed earlier: cost, quality, and access. Making this translation is a significant challenge for senior management in health care, because the past is not necessarily prologue to the future. Reengineering is often overlooked as a means of creating all new market positions.

We have said in our definition that key capabilities are the result of focusing on an organization's core processes. We now turn to the definition of *core process.*

## Core Process

*A group of interrelated, measurable, cross-functional business processes that creates an output valued by the customer.*

The most important word in the lexicon of reengineering is *process.* As our definition indicates, processes can come in different types. The fourth step to be taken by the senior executives involves the identification of the core processes that are critical to creating a key capability.

Recall our earlier discussion of the traditional vertical functions within a business structure. We said that coordination across several cross-functional areas is required to meet a customer's request. The path taken to connect these areas is called a core process.[12] The actual number of core processes in any given business tends to be relatively small—you rarely find more than six to ten in any single organization.

The reason *core process* is such a strange-sounding concept is that we have rarely looked at our organizations in this manner. Generally, we have trained ourselves to think in terms of functional areas and to accept that the value and purpose of such delineations is the focused expertise and professional development that are possible within each specific area. It has become a truism that within reengineering efforts the most difficult task many encounter is coming to recognize and understand what their core processes are.

The first step in making processes more visible and understandable is to label them in a way that expresses their beginning and end states. In this way, we could create a sort of Rosetta stone to help us make the translation. The following are examples:

- **Product development** becomes "concept to prototype."
- **Sales** becomes "prospect to order."
- **Order fulfillment** becomes "order to payment."
- **Manufacturing** becomes "procurement to shipment."
- **Service** becomes "inquiry to resolution."

Naming a process is less important than understanding the dependencies it creates among organizational functions. As our definition indicates, it is also critical that core processes (and business processes) are measurable—particularly in terms that are of value to a customer. The senior executives bear a significant responsibility for the selection of the core processes, an output that will set the stage for work done subsequently by reengineering teams.

The teams that redesign the core processes will discover that redesign must overcome a fundamental problem—managing "the white space" between functional areas. It is precisely this problem that becomes so apparent to one's customers—and competitors. The teams will also find that it is necessary to understand their customers' and vendors' processes, since redesign efforts generally result in processes that interface with them. In fact, a customer represents the process that receives the output from another process.

We will return to the discussion of processes in Chapter 5, when we examine specific examples that occur in the health care industry. For now, we turn our attention to the final step in the executive staircase—business processes.

## Business Process

> *A group of measurable linked activities that transforms an*
> *input into an output valued by the customer.*

Although we show the identification of business processes as
the fifth and final executive step, this step is often an exception.
When senior teams do choose to pursue it, their outcomes are
generally more suggestive than prescriptive. By the time they get
to this level, they are dealing with a body of knowledge that
one would only expect to be accessible at lower levels in the
organization. In fairness, we should say that some executive teams
draw on staff to help them move through all of the steps we have
reviewed.

As our definition indicates, business processes operate at the
transactional level of an organization. Many confuse the scope
of a business process with the work performed within a given
functional area. In fact, business processes are invisible to most
people, as are core processes, because they often spread across
several functions and are obscured by the organization's structural
boundaries. In addition to not being seen, these processes have
no owner or "manager." The whole end-to-end activity is the
responsibility of no one!

Some people have difficulty discerning a business process from
its underlying activities. Admittedly, this can become a game of
infinite regress in the abstract. On a day-to-day basis, however,
this is not a terribly difficult issue. People who perform the work
find it easy to explain the difference. But another issue does have
more relevance: Are all processes visible to a customer? The answer
is no. There are managerial processes and supporting processes
that are focused on the internal operations of any organization.
For our purposes, we refer to business processes as value-adding
because they are visible to customers.

Consider the process we called "product development" (or
"concept to prototype"). It could consist of the following business
processes:

- Research and target marketing
- Collaborative development/design
- Advertising and promotions
- Product setup and testing
- Product evaluation.

Each of these business processes could be rephrased in terms of
the breadth of activities they contain. Looking more specifically
at the health care industry, let us consider an example that helps

demonstrate the hierarchy we have created: key capability, core process, and business process.

The top executives of a health care organization have developed a vision that requires a specific key capability to help them gain competitive advantage. Further, they have identified a core process and one of its business processes that serve to support this capability. The key capability is *integrated service delivery*; the core process is *diagnostics to accounting*; the business process is *scheduling*. The executives initially called the core process *outpatient services* but later chose a label that described the front-to-end business processes within it. They also identified *scheduling* as one of the business processes within the core process. The reengineering team selected by the executives later changed the name of this business process to *contact to arrival*.

We can see from the steps taken by executives that reengineering is tightly tied to the organization's future direction and objectives. In a later chapter, we will show how an executive group creates a governing structure for the reengineering effort and assigns teams to redesign selected core processes.

## REENGINEERING PRINCIPLES

Organizations that fail at reengineering do so because they ignore the principles behind it. They are often *aware* of the principles, but they convince themselves that their unique situation protects them from the negative results of violating them. This absurd logic is often captured in the "Dilbert" cartoons by Scott Adams.[13] Perhaps every organization has the management it deserves.

Some people argue that many of the reengineering principles are no different from those for other approaches, and in some instances this is true. However, taken together, the principles of reengineering help define an approach that is different—and certainly more demanding—than others. Table 2.1 offers a list of these principles.

1. **Strategy drives reengineering and senior managers lead it.**
   Our previous discussion has underscored the responsibilities of senior management for linking reengineering to strategy. In Chapter 3, we will provide a detailed description of the leadership roles and responsibilities of senior managers within a reengineering effort.

2. **Focus on value to the customer.** Reengineering goes beyond increasing customer satisfaction. It seeks to fundamentally alter the customer relationship to deliver value in a way that neither party considered possible.

**Table 2.1** Reengineering Principles

| | |
|---|---|
| • Strategy drives reengineering | • Reengineering is organization's top priority |
| • Senior managers lead reengineering | |
| • Focus on value to customer | • Align organizational infrastructure |
| • Focus on cross-organizational processes | • Embed information technology as enabler within the process |
| • Eliminate, integrate, compress processes | |
| • Organize around outcomes, not tasks | • Capture data once at the source |
| • Metrics make the difference | • Process designers inherit their efforts |
| | • Stealth reengineering is a myth |

3. **Focus on cross-organizational processes.** The business literature has often obscured the fact that a large percentage of so-called reengineering projects are limited by functional interests and responsibilities. If an organization is not addressing cross-functional processes, it is not reengineering.

4. **Eliminate, integrate, and compress processes.** Among the primary outcomes of reengineering are removing non-value-adding tasks and doing what needs to be done faster, and with fewer resources.

5. **Organize around outcomes, not tasks.** We have said that the scope of work crosses functional lines, but the organization's structure does not reflect this. Rather, boundaries are drawn around groups of functionally defined activities. Reengineering calls for structural redesign that more closely follows the path of the core process.

6. **Metrics make the difference.** The classic slogan "you get what you measure" was never truer than it is in reengineering. Reengineering demands new measures that are process-focused and that reflect dramatically increased expectations for performance—performance that is impossible to attain through current processes.

7. **Reengineering is the organization's top priority.** You can't make revolution your third priority. If a health care organization chooses to pursue reengineering, it must devote to it nothing less than its full attention. Otherwise, it will be forced to compete for resources

as though it were a "nice to do" program instead of the way to reposition the organization. For those who believe that—insisting that serving patients in the top priority is a presumptuous request, consider this analogy: What is the top priority of an opera singer in a burning theater?

8. **Align the organizational infrastructure.** Early reengineering efforts often overlooked the need to go beyond the redesign of processes. Redesign must receive support in the form of budgets, people, time, and other resources. Organizations often find that making infrastructure changes is at least as difficult as process redesign itself.

*You can't make revolution your third priority.*

9. **Embed change management and information technology as enablers of the process.** Reengineering will serve as a catalyst to large-scale organization change. Those who attempt it find that the "soft stuff" turns out to be the "hard stuff." Resistance needs to be anticipated, treated as normal, and dealt with openly and directly. Otherwise, the organization risks sending a signal that it doesn't support change. Further, our discussion of disappointments associated with the use of information technology points to the need to rethink how technology can allow a redesign option to succeed. Again, its role is to enable—not drive—the process redesign.

10. **Capture data and quality once, at the source.** It is nearly impossible to escape having to submit redundant information in order to obtain medical care. Reengineering calls for redesigning process so that data can be captured once—the first time it is needed—and is made available in multiple formats thereafter. Related to this is the need to ensure that the desired quality of materials and service is determined at the beginning of the pipeline of activity—not as a checkpoint after the fact.

11. **Process designers inherit their efforts.** The Vikings had it right. When they landed, their ships were burned—underscoring their mission to succeed. Reengineering offers a unique opportunity for a radical redesign of processes, and those who are asked to build this new environment should be asked to live in it. Separating the architects from the inhabitants loses this sense of accountability.

12. **Stealth reengineering is a myth.** You cannot expect to reengineer covertly—even those who have been successful claim they should have communicated more to their organization. Communication comes in the form of executive education on reengineering as well as the media we know

exists within an organization. One cannot communicate too much during a reengineering effort.

## THE ROLE OF ENABLERS

Early reengineering advocates found that what distinguished reengineering from other approaches was the use of information technology to enable process redesign. A subsequent "lesson learned" was that managing the change brought about through reengineering was critical to getting the redesign accepted and implemented.

### Information Technology

The unfortunate track record associated with the acquisition and application of information technology makes it hard to persuade people of its importance within reengineering. Technology per se is not at fault. It has always been capable of making things happen faster—including dumb things. It should not be blamed for the decision to apply it to processes that were suboptimal in the first place.

Later we will examine more fully the enabling role of information technology within reengineering. For now, it is important to state uncategorically that the full potential of reengineering is realized by using technology to break old rules and by allowing businesses to do things that no one ever considered or thought possible.

The use of information technology as an enabler, however, does not justify the sunk cost of investment dollars. Rather, experts who understand the capacity of technology must use this knowledge to inform the creative redesign process. Or, as some have said, technology first creates the problem, then solves it.

### Change Management

We identified four key dimensions of an organization that must be addressed simultaneously to ensure successful change: leadership, workforce, structure, and process. The business literature provides numerous examples of organizations whose success hinged on following this advice. In Chapter 7 we will explore how change management needs to be embedded within a reengineering effort. But for now, it will suffice to say that a pattern of change management activity among successful organizations includes these elements:

- Articulating why the change is necessary
- Addressing technical, political, and cultural resistance

- Redesigning the organizations boundaries
- Using "social architecting" in the placement of people, changes in work space, and creating new networks of interaction.[14]

## AGGRESSIVE METRICS

One of the primary drivers within reengineering is the demand for a level of performance that most people believe is unattainable. And they are correct. It is absolutely impossible if one pursues such goals with the organization's existing mindset and processes. But "unreasonable" demands lead to discussions of options that would never have been considered otherwise. Here are two examples:

- Northern Telecom's senior management established a complex and difficult goal: create and implement a revolutionized order flow process that would decrease the time between customer need and final bill by 75 percent within two years.[15]
- Motorola's CEO set the performance standards that drove the company to its stand on quality and cycle time. Specifically, he wanted Motorola to reduce manufacturing defects by 90 percent every two years and cycle time—the time required for tasks such as filling a customer's order or developing a new product—by 90 percent every five years. By 1993, Motorola achieved a defect rate of 3.4 per million parts—down from 6,000![16]

We have seen other organizations set "stretch goals" such as these:

- Double customer service satisfaction levels in two years.
- Reduce new drug development cycle time by 50 percent in three years.
- Reduce involuntary employee turnover to 10 percent by the end of the next fiscal year.
- Reduce processing costs for customer orders by 60 percent over three years.
- Reduce operating costs by 50 percent within six months.
- Ninety percent of all patients will be seen within 15 minutes of their scheduled appointment time.

Chapter 3 will provide several examples of performance improvements within the health care industry that reflect this call for revolutionary thinking. The industry is coming to terms with its own shift in metrics and is using it as a major impetus within reengineering.

## ROLE OF TOOLS AND METHODOLOGY

One of the challenges of reengineering is a very personal one—coming to terms with one's own lack of understanding of the concept and how to apply it. Human nature being what it is, most of us deal with the discomfort of ignorance through denial. "It is probably something I already know—or don't need to." We construct a fantasy about how much we know—how similar a new thing is to an old thing—and underestimate the preparation needed to address the demand.

Reengineering does draw on other techniques and approaches that many of us have used before. Unfortunately, this familiarity masks something about reengineering that we need to deal with directly. Reengineering requires new knowledge that comes in the form of tools and methodology.

### Tools

There are specific tools that support the work performed by a process team. However, many people assume that a tool used elsewhere can simply be applied to reengineering without much modification. This turns out not to be the case in many instances. For example, how does a *process* vision differ from a *corporate* vision? Do you benchmark processes in the same way you benchmark companies? The work done by process teams demands tools specifically designed to help them.

### Methodology

In a nation that reads the instructions when all else fails, it is not surprising that many people pursue reengineering in a similar manner. The result is what I call a "random walk" or "improvisation with feedback." Of course, this generally leads to confusion, frustration, and suboptimal outcomes. As our model for process reengineering will point out, this is very demanding and complex work. To perform it, teams need to have a road map to guide them.

*Smaller players may find themselves compelled to reengineer because the larger organizations they depend on are changing the rules of the game.*

This should not be confused with a rigidly prescribed "cookbook" that lays out a specific sequence of activities. Rather, it offers a framework, within which teams can tailor their efforts to meet the organization's goals—without having to start completely from scratch. Reengineering teams have used a variety of models and methodologies to guide them, all of which have served to keep the effort on track, offer suggestions on how to sequence the work, and reassure sponsors that resources are being used in an effective manner.

## IMPLICATIONS FOR HEALTH CARE ············

We conclude our overview of reengineering by highlighting implications for the health care industry. Although subsequent chapters will pursue these implications in far more detail, some worth emphasizing follow.

### Size of the Organization

Many in the industry have concluded that reengineering is only appropriate for larger organizations. However, reengineering is now being done in smaller and smaller organizations. It may actually be easier in smaller organizations because their bureaucracies are not as entrenched and because more people are directly in contact with customers. Further, smaller players may find themselves compelled to reengineer because the larger organizations they depend on are changing the rules of the game. That is, larger organizations use reengineering to achieve the flexibility once associated with their smaller competitors—thus forcing smaller organizations to take steps to regain their edge.

### Short-Term Opportunities

Most health care companies are facing financial constraints and cannot afford a long-term improvement effort with benefits that accrue only at the end. Reengineering teams find short-term opportunities within the effort that bring substantial benefit before the business processes are redesigned. We will discuss this more in the "process fast-path" section of our *process reengineering* model. For now, we should simply note that short-term opportunities often focus on cost reduction, a paramount issue within the industry.

### Clinical Applications

It is important to recognize that reengineering can be applied to clinical processes as well as practice management processes. In a later chapter, we will offer a *business reengineering* model that makes clear that a reengineering effort requires careful attention to the creation of a governing structure and team selection. This kind of leadership is particularly important if separate efforts are made to redesign clinical and practice management processes.

## The Current Environment

We are already aware of some telltale signs that reengineering is badly needed in the health care industry. These include the following:

- Declining profit margins
- High levels of patient dissatisfaction
- Threatened physician revenue
- Inability to compete effectively for managed care contracts.

## Health Care Processes

Reengineering has process as its focal point, but many health care administrators believe it is too difficult to identify processes in their own organizations. A later chapter will describe several core processes in health care and their supporting business processes. Some of the processes that have already been the focus of reengineering efforts are rehabilitation, support services, intensive care therapeutics, diagnostics, coronary care therapeutics, and admissions.

## Capitation

The advent of global capitation underscores the need to address internal factors that affect the capitation rate. Targets for reengineering under these circumstances include the following:

- Efficiency and cost controls
- Nonphysician staff to provide care
- Ability to control specialist or ancillary utilization
- Administrative costs that include information, claims processing, utilization tracking
- Redesign of clinical processes to achieve desired outcomes more efficiently.

Any new approach to gaining organizational performance should be compared to alternatives. Our next chapter will look at how reengineering compares to other approaches to organizational change.

## SUMMARY

Reengineering calls for a radical redesign of business processes to achieve dramatic improvement in performance. Although many organizations claim to be doing reengineering, surveys find that fewer than half actually attempt to redesign business processes. This creates a paradox: reengineering is popular, but it more often results in failure than success. It is likely that many of these failures are mislabeled as reengineering efforts.

To understand reengineering requires acknowledging it as a form of large-scale organization change. Four key dimensions of the organization must be managed simultaneously to achieve successful change: leadership, workforce, structure, and process. Focusing solely on the process dimension is not sufficient to achieve dramatic performance improvements.

To many people, reengineering appears to be altogether new, but its roots actually trace back to Frederick W. Taylor's study of scientific management. Three fields that grew out of Taylor's work combine to form the reengineering approach: industrial engineering, organizational and behavioral theory, and information and measurement systems.

A basic tenet of reengineering is that organizational inefficiency results from fragmented processes and the creation of services performed by specialists. The vertical structures in many organizations are the target for reengineering's charge to focus on the horizontal linkages of processes that cross functional boundaries. Few people recognize this horizontal path, and often no one bears responsible for orchestrating these processes.

To gain the performance improvements promised from reengineering, the organization's senior team must take responsibility for setting the stage for the effort. The major steps they need to pursue include setting a future vision, agreeing on a strategy to achieve this vision, deciding on key capabilities that form the basis of the strategy, and identifying the core processes and business processes that need to be redesigned. Without a strong linkage to the organization's strategy, reengineering will not receive the leadership and support needed to reach its objectives.

The success of reengineering depends on an organization's ability to understand and adhere to the main principles. Making reengineering the organization's top priority and ensuring that it receives support and leadership from the top executive team are among the most important of these principles. Understanding how to use information technology and the management of change to enable the redesign and implementation of business processes are also of prime importance.

Successful reengineering requires new measures of performance that reflect the desire for a dramatic improvement beyond what is possible by doing business as usual. The teams charged with the responsibility for redesign will need tools designed for this effort and a methodology to guide them.

Although health care organizations are only beginning to turn to reengineering, they will soon see the implications for the industry. Reengineering can be applied to organizations of various sizes, and it offers the opportunity to gain short-term improvements (e.g., cost reduction) as well as the long-term benefits of process redesign. Both clinical and practice management processes can be improved through reengineering, and currently there are signs, like declining profit margins, that both kinds of processes need it.

## Notes

1. For more details on the costs and failures associated with reengineering, see B. Caldwell, 1994, "Missteps, Miscues," *InformationWeek*, (20 June): 38–44.

2. See M. Hammer and J. Champy, 1993, *Reengineering the Corporation* (New York: Harper Business), for a description of the elements of this definition and additional reengineering information.

3. M. M. Klein, 1994, cites a 1992 survey of CEOs in his article, "The Most Fatal Reengineering Mistakes," *Information Strategy* (Summer): 21–28.

4. A review of this research can be found in G. D. Kissler, 1991, *The Change Riders* (Reading, MA: Addison-Wesley). Despite the extensive body of research demonstrating the need to address all four of the dimensions described here, proponents continue to push for their "favorite." For example, one claim is that "deep and meaningful involvement of the whole organization will lead naturally to a new organizational order." See T. Brown, 1994, "Deengineering the Corporation," *Industry Week* 243 (18 April): 18–26.

5. For additional details, see D. Rigby, 1993, "The Secret History of Process Reengineering," *Planning Review* (March–April): 24–26; A. Gabor, 1990, *The Man Who Discovered Quality* (New York: Random House); D. Ciampa, 1992, *Total Quality: A User's Guide for Implementation* (Reading, MA: Addison-Wesley); W. A. Pasmore, 1988, *Designing Effective Organizations: The Sociotechnical Systems Approach* (New York: Wiley); E. Trist and K. Bamforth, 1951, "Some Social and Psychological Consequences of the Longwall Method of Coal-Getting," *Human Relations* 6 (1): 3–38; E. Mayo, 1977, *The Human Problems of Industrial Civilization* (New York: Arno Press); D. F. Noble, 1986, *Forces of Production: A Social History of Industrial Automation* (New York: Oxford University Press); S. Zuboff, 1988, *In the Age of the Smart Machine* (New York: Basic Books); E. E. Lawler, 1988, *High-Involvement Management* (San Francisco: Jossey-Bass); and A. Toffler, 1980, *The Third Wave* (New York: Telecom Library).

6. A particularly good discussion on this topic can be found in G. A. Rummler and A. P. Brache, 1990, *Improving Performance* (San Francisco, Jossey-Bass).

7. J. R. Galbraith, 1994, offers a thorough review of the benefits from a lateral organization structure in his book, *Competing with Flexible Lateral Organizations* (Reading, MA: Addison-Wesley). Also see J. A. Byrne, 1993, "The Horizontal Corporation," *Business Week* 20 December, 76–81; and F. Ostroff and D. Smith, 1992, "Redesigning the Corporation: The Horizontal Organization," (New York: McKinsey & Company). The issue of shifting to a horizontal view of business processes actually has an enormous implication behind it. Drawn to its natural conclusion, it means actually "destroying" the vertical structure as it is now known. I find it interesting, nonetheless, that many executives continue to be "surprised" at what they get from reengineering efforts in which this goal becomes understood by "culture carriers." For an example, see J. King, 1994, "Re-engineering Slammed," *Computerworld* 28 (13 June): 1, 14.

8. J. A. Pearce II and F. Davis, 1987, cite research supporting this point in "Corporate Mission Statements: The Bottom Line," *Academy of Management Executive* (May): 109–16.

9. See G. Stalk, Jr., and T. M. Hout, 1990, *Competing against Time* (New York: The Free Press) for a more detailed review of the change in strategic thinking over this period. Stalk, 1993, offers insight into why focusing on cycle time is not enough in his article, "Japan's Dark Side of Time," *Harvard Business Review* 71 (July–August): 93–102. P. R. Thomas, 1990, is another proponent of the time-based strategy and offers a detailed description of this approach in his two books, *Competitiveness through Total Cycle Time* (New York: McGraw-Hill) and 1991, *Getting Competitive* (New York: McGraw-Hill). A recent description of the use of speed as a competitive strategy in businesses can be found in W. M. Bulkeley, 1994, "The Latest Big Thing at Many Companies Is Speed, Speed, Speed," *The Wall Street Journal*, 23 December.

10. P. J. H. Schoemaker, 1992, offers insights into how this is accomplished in his article, "How to Link Strategic Vision to Core Capabilities," *Sloan Management Review* (Fall): 67–81.

11. A treatment of the "capability" side of this debate can be found in G. Stalk, Jr., P. Evans, and L. E. Shulman, 1992, "Competing on Capabilities: The New Rules of Corporate Strategy," *Harvard Business Review* 70 (March–April): 57–69. The "competency" perspective can be found in C. K. Prahalad and G. Hamel, 1990, "The Competence of the Corporation," *Harvard Business Review* 68 (May–June): 79–91.

12. Several sources have offered insights into how to identify and understand processes within organizations. In addition to the Hammer and Champy book cited in note 2, see T. H. Davenport, 1993, *Process Innovation* (Boston: Harvard Business School Press); H. J. Johansson, P. McHugh, A. J. Pendlebury, and W. A. Wheeler III, 1993, *Business Process Reengineering* (New York: John Wiley);

and J. N. Lowenthal, 1994, *Reengineering the Organization: A Step-by-Step Approach to Corporate Revitalization* (Milwaukee, WI: ASQC Quality Press).

13. For a truly hysterical and insightful treatment of the insanity that passes for normal business behavior, I would recommend two books by S. Adams: 1991, *Build a Better Life by Stealing Office Supplies* (New York: Topper Books) and 1989, *Always Postpone Meetings with Time-Wasting Morons* (New York: Topper Books).

14. A fairly recent discussion of this topic can be found in N. M. Tichy, 1993, "Revolutionize Your Company," *Fortune* (13 December): 114–18.

15. The Northern Telecom example is described in G. M. Palmer and G. S. Burns, 1993, "Revolutionizing the Business: Strategies for Succeeding with Change," *Human Resource Planning* 15, (1): 77–84.

16. The information cited on Motorola can be found in C. Hill and K. Yamada, 1992, "Staying Power: Motorola Illustrates How an Aged Giant Can Remain Vibrant," *The Wall Street Journal*, 9 December.

## CHAPTER 3

# A Matter of Choice

*Inaction speaks louder than words.*

Anonymous

**A**NYONE WHO suggests reengineering as an option, and gets no resistance, must be in a room by themselves. The typical chorus of dissent comes from those wanting to avoid change and those who prefer another approach. The first group is made up of people with legitimate concerns; the latter is intent on sabotage. We will discuss both in Chapter 7. This chapter will compare reengineering to several alternatives and provide examples of performance outcomes achieved through reengineering.

## FAIR COMPARISONS

It is only fair that those of us who promote reengineering should bear the responsiblity for distinguishing it from other approaches.[1] As the incumbent in such an arena, it stands at a disadvantage. It has yet to gain the advantage of name recognition. More space in the business literature is allocated to alternatives. Most important, however, is that those who have made a commitment to other approaches severely resist reengineering—sometimes for political reasons. Debates among proponents of different approaches tend to overemphasize their differences and downplay similarities. A wide range of criteria can help to clarify the commonalities and contrasts between reengineering and these other approaches. These criteria include the following:

- **Role of process:** The degree of emphasis placed on business process
- **Focus of change:** The type of change the approach pursues
- **Key assumption:** The fundamental underlying premise for the approach
- **Output/input goal:** The expected change in production and resource requirements resulting from the approach
- **Scope:** The breadth of activity considered within the domain of the approach
- **Primary target:** The overall objective being sought
- **Key enabler:** The primary form of assistance used to achieve results
- **Duration:** The relative time frame associated with achieving results
- **Direction:** The typical origin of leadership for the approach
- **Risk:** The level of risk associated with the approach
- **Infrastructure change:** The degree to which the organization's supporting infrastructure is required to change to achieve results
- **Improvement goal:** The percentage of organizational improvement that can be expected from using the approach.

These criteria will be used to compare reengineering to five other performance improvement approaches: total quality management (TQM)/continuous quality improvement (CQI), employee involvement, sociotechnical systems (STS), downsizing, and automation.[2] Tables 3.1 and 3.2 summarize these comparisons.

## Comparing Reengineering and TQM/CQI

### Role of Process

Both approaches focus primarily on process. In fact, many organizations with TQM/CQI experience have concluded that this commonality helped them transition to reengineering.

### Focus of Change

A major point of departure is in existing processes. While TQM/CQI seeks to improve current processes, reengineering looks for a more radical redesign.

**Table 3.1**  Comparisons among Reengineering, TQM/CQI, and Employee Involvement

|  | Reengineering | TQM/CQI | Employee Involvement |
|---|---|---|---|
| Role of process | Primary | Primary | Ignored |
| Focus of change | Radical process innovation | Incremental quality improvement | Organizational design |
| Key assumption | Clean slate | Current processes acceptable | Ineffective organization |
| Output/input goal | More with less | More with more | More with same |
| Scope | Broad (cross-function) | Narrow (within function) | Narrow (within function) |
| Primary target | Customer relationship | Customer satisfaction | Internal work environment |
| Key enabler | Information technology | Statistical control | Enrichment and workteams |
| Duration | Short | Long | Long |
| Direction | Top-down | Bottom-up | Self-management |
| Risk | High | Moderate | Low |
| Infrastructure change | Critical | Minimal | Critical |
| Improvement goal | 50–100% | 10–15% | ? |

## Key Assumption

TQM/CQI accepts current processes, but reengineering starts with a clean slate. That is, improving current processes is viewed as a waste of effort. The notion of a "clean slate" is not always taken literally in reengineering, yet there is a deliberate effort *not* to try to fix things that should be scrapped.

## Output/Input Goal

A point of some contention is the way an organization should align its output-to-input ratio. The proponents of reengineering claim that the organization will be capable of increasing its output with a reduced level of resources. The business media have pointed out that this often translates into layoffs. TQM/CQI also claims that performance will increase, but it appears that increases in resources are required to develop and maintain the quality effort itself. In some cases, this is due to added process steps associated with quality measurement and analysis.

*TQM/CQI accepts current processes, but reengineering starts with a clean slate.*

**Table 3.2** Comparisons among Reengineering, STS, Downsizing, and Automation

| | Reengineering | STS | Downsizing | Automation |
|---|---|---|---|---|
| Role of process | Primary | Primary | Ignored | Ignored |
| Focus of change | Radical process innovation | Incremental process improvement | Cost reduction | Cost: down; Speed: up |
| Key assumption | Clean slate | Poor sociotechnical alignment | Too many people | Inefficient data use |
| Output/input goal | More with less | More with same | Same with less | More with same |
| Scope | Broad (cross-function) | Narrow (within function) | Moderate | Moderate |
| Primary target | Customer relationship | Outputs and specifications | Headcount reduction | Data management |
| Key enabler | Information technology | Variance analysis | Removal of personnel | Information technology |
| Duration | Short | Moderate | Moderate | Long |
| Direction | Top-down | Bottom-up | Top-down | Middle-out |
| Risk | High | Low | High | Moderate |
| Infrastructure change | Critical | Moderate | Ignore | Moderate |
| Improvement goal | 50–100% | 10–15% | ? | ? |

## Scope

It is quite typical to find TQM/CQI efforts within existing business functions. Reengineering, by design, crosses functional lines, so its scope is considerably broader.

## Primary Target

The primary objective of the quality movement is to meet customer needs in such a way as to delight them (i.e., increase satisfaction). In reengineering, customer satisfaction is a by-product—an outcome that results from a radical change in the relationship between the organization and its customers. The ATM solution described in Chapter 2 is an example.

## Key Enabler

Reengineering turns to information technology as a key enabler of redesign. The primary enabler for TQM/CQI is statistical control. Reengineering and TQM/CQI both draw heavily on change management to enable the changes they seek.

## Duration

It has become almost a truism that continuous improvement requires a relatively long time to demonstrate a quantum change in performance. A range of three to five years is quite common. Reengineering tends to focus on a much shorter period—approximately 12 months.

## Direction

TQM/CQI pursues a bottom-up approach through the training of teams of people at fairly low levels in an organization. These teams seek ways to reduce process variation and sustain continuous performance improvement. Reengineering, in contrast, is driven from the top of the organization. The reason for this is that it crosses functional lines, and the authority to do this resides at the top of the organization. Further, it would be impossible to obtain organizational consensus for the magnitude of change (or disruption) to the status quo that results from reengineering. Therefore, reengineering needs to be linked to the strategic repositioning of the organization, a responsibility belonging to the most senior level of management.

## Risk

Because of its scope and target, reengineering carries far more risk than TQM/CQI. Reengineering risk also comes from the degree to which the organization's infrastructure must be changed to support the process change.

### Infrastructure Change

TQM/CQI requires a moderate amount of realignment, often in the form of educational support and allocation of work schedules to allow for team-based work sessions. Reengineering, on the other hand, makes a substantially greater demand for the alignment of the organization's infrastructure. It requires changes in skill mix, recruiting criteria, performance measures, career paths, pay systems, budgetary allocation, and the redesign of organization structure, just to mention a few.

### Improvement Goal

Finally, the majority of TQM/CQI efforts yield a 10 to 15 percent rate of performance improvement. For organizations that have experienced a negative trend, this is a significant accomplishment. Reengineering stands out, however, because it eschews this level of improvement, choosing instead to pursue improvement in the range of 50 to 100 percent. Examples of even higher levels can be cited, but even the more conservative numbers reflect a sharp break with past expectations. In fact, it is precisely this extreme level of expectation that serves as a catalyst for redesigning versus improving current processes.

We will return to a discussion of these two approaches later to consider the relationship between the two as organizations go through different periods of change.

## Comparing Reengineering and Employee Involvement

### Role of Process

The role of process, which is primary within reengineering, is not integral to employee involvement. Rather, employee involvement seeks to change the relationship between employees and the organization.

### Focus of Change

Employee involvement is focused on organization design, whereas reengineering seeks radical process innovation.

### Key Assumption

Employee involvement assumes that the organization's ineffectiveness results from the lack of input from people capable of offering useful suggestions for improvement. Reengineering assumes that current business processes should be scrapped, including those pertaining to communication.

## Output/Input Goal

Employee involvement promises performance improvement but generally leaves resource levels unchanged. Reengineering promises increased performance with fewer resources.

## Scope

Compared to the broad cross-functional scope of reengineering, employee involvement—like TQM/CQI—tends to occur within existing organizational functions.

## Primary Target

Employee involvement is an inwardly focused approach, deliberately attempting to improve the work environment, whereas both reengineering and TQM/CQI focus on the customer.

## Key Enabler

Employee involvement draws heavily upon the enrichment of jobs (increasing perceived value through changes in autonomy, feedback, and so on) and team participation. Information technology and change management are the key enablers within reengineering. There is some gray area here, however.[3] One could argue that the use of redesign teams is quite similar to the use of teams within employee involvment. The difference becomes apparent when one examines the teams' charters. Employee involvement teams are generally restricted to one area of the business. Reengineering teams have license to move across the organization.

## Duration

It is not uncommon for an employee involvement effort to have a three- to five-year time frame. Reengineering usually occurs in about a year. Reengineering implementation is likely to take more than a year, but the objective is to seek tangible benefits within the one-year time frame.

## Direction

Reengineering teams are sanctioned and chosen by top management, and redesign is linked to changes in business strategy. Employee involvement teams tend to involve relatively lower-level employees who focus on more transactional issues. Top management may be aware of their existence, but the "champion" is generally found lower in an organization.

### Risk

Due to its scope and transactional focus, employee involvement presents less risk for an organization than does reengineering. Employee participation calls for organizational adjustment; reengineering calls for a radical shift in core processes.

### Infrastructure Change

Both approaches call for a major realignment of the organization's infrastructure. For employee involvement, policies and practices are altered to support a team-based work environment. Reengineering looks for a broader base of alignment as well.

### Improvement Goal

The performance improvements associated with employee involvement are difficult to state with confidence, because the results are often anecdotal and intangible. Reengineering stands out because of its promise of improvements in the 50–100 percent range.

## Comparing Reengineering and Sociotechnical Systems (STS)

### Role of Process

Both approaches have process as their primary focus.

### Focus of Change/Key Assumption

STS tends to seek improvement of existing processes. This improvement is aimed at the poor alignment between the social and technical aspects of how work is performed. Reengineering calls for a radical change, generally requiring completely new processes. Therefore, STS would result in an improvement trend that is less dramatic and disruptive than what one would expect from reengineering.

### Output/Input Goal

The STS realignment of the social and technical sides of work allows for an increase in performance without requiring additional resources. Reengineering seeks improvement and a reduced resource requirement.

### Scope

STS is focused most often on processes within a business function. Reengineering has a broader scope, seeking process changes that cross functional lines.

## Primary Target

While reengineering works to change the relationship between customers and the organization, STS looks for changes in performance outcomes tied to the development of new work specifications.

## Key Enabler

The key enabler for STS is variance analysis, a technique originating in industrial engineering. Its purpose is to identify portions of a process that create a cascade of problems due to performance outside an accepted range. Reengineering draws heavily on information technology to enable process redesign. Both use change management to support process changes. STS is synonymous with many of change management's principles; reengineering has only recently begun to embrace them.

*There is a big difference between reengineering and a deliberate effort to reduce jobs.*

## Duration

The typical 12-month reengineering effort is much shorter than what is required for STS. An STS approach, like TQM/CQI, measures its life span in years.

## Direction

Another similarity between STS and the quality approaches is the bottom-up orientation. Teams of people are trained in problem solving and the STS techniques. They offer suggestions mostly to middle-level management. Reengineering is a top-down effort, and teams have greater access and accountability to top management.

## Risk

It is understandable that STS poses little risk, compared to reengineering. Its changes are usually contained within a functional area, and it does not seek to redefine the customer relationship.

## Infrastructure Change

STS requires less infrastructure change than reengineering, and most of the change occurs within the domain of a single business function. For example, STS would not generally request organizationwide changes in compensation just to accommodate the needs of a single business function. Reengineering's scope would be likely to result in just such a request.

## Improvement Goal

STS has been described (inaccurately) as reengineering without the assistance of information technology. The use of information technology does occur within STS, but it tends to be late in the effort. The absence (or delay) of information processing is only part of the distinction between STS and reengineering. The history of STS tends to be associated with increases in performance that range from 10 to 15 percent.

## Comparing Reengineering and Downsizing

One of the criticisms of reengineering is that it is just a cleverly disguised means of producing layoffs.[4] It is certainly no secret that organizations have been trying to reduce costs for over a decade, often by removing positions that were no longer deemed necessary. However, there is a big difference between reengineering and a deliberate effort to reduce jobs (downsizing).

### Role of Process

Reengineering seeks to change business processes, but downsizing ignores the work and focuses instead on those performing it.

### Focus of Change

The primary change that downsizing seeks is cost reduction. Reengineering looks for a radical form of process innovation. Such innovation often leads to cost reduction because of improved efficiency and a reduced need for resources.

### Key Assumption

Those pursuing downsizing assume that the cost problem is the result of employing too many people. Reengineering starts with the premise that the problem is processes that are not worth improving.

### Output/Input Goal

The reengineering goal is to gain improvement in performance and reduce the demand for resources, whereas downsizing tries to sustain the current performance level with fewer people.

### Scope

Aside from some "on death's door" scenarios, downsizing tends to be fairly selective and often occurs within a specific functional area. It is common for an organization to outsource activity it sees as outside its primary business direction. This could include legal departments, training departments, and so on. Reengineering looks at change across many, if not all, functional areas.

### Primary Target

The target for reengineering is a change in customer relationships; downsizing seeks a reduction in head count.

## Key Enabler

It is easy to see that the key enabler for downsizing is the removal of personnel. Information technology and change management are reengineering's enablers.

## Duration

Downsizing tends to occur over a moderately long period of time. Most organizations will attempt to reduce staff through normal attrition and early retirement packages. More aggressive tactics take two to three years, and sometimes longer. A recent change in human resources executives at IBM suggests that patience is wearing thin for this kind of time frame. Reengineering efforts yield results within 12 months but can take longer to achieve full implementation of redesigned processes.

## Direction/Risk

There is some common ground between these two approaches. Both are driven by top management and both present a high degree of risk. Top management drives reengineering because of its cross-functional scope. Downsizing is driven from the top because, tactically, voluntary unemployment has significant limitations. Involuntary separations, on the other hand, can become a form of "organizational liposuction" that inadvertently removes more brains than fat.[5] The primary risk in reengineering is the radical change in business direction toward new market relationships.

## Infrastructure Change

The organizational infrastructure is left largely intact throughout a downsizing effort, with an obvious increase in resources needed to process the exiting of people. Reengineering, by comparison, creates a substantial demand for realignment of the organization's support infrastructure. This ranges from shifts in the recruiting and selection approach to achieve a different skill mix, to developing process-based performance measures, to the introduction of team-based compensation systems.

## Improvement Goal

There is doubt about what improvements, if any, can be claimed by downsizing. Organizations such as General Electric found that removing people without changing the way work was performed just contributed to the loss of the mobile survivors and lower morale among the rest. The increased productivity that follows a downsizing announcement cannot be sustained indefinitely. At some point the survivors become aware that they now face the organizational equivalent of nuclear winter. By comparison, reengineering offers an increase in performance that reaches levels of 50 to 100 percent, and sometimes greater. The critical difference is that improvement comes from changing the work processes— not the job incumbents. Layoffs can occur when a reengineering effort streamlines work and removes non-value-adding tasks, but the choice to retrain or reposition employees remains. Downsizing rarely offers such latitude.

## Comparing Reengineering and Automation

### Role of Process

Automation tends to ignore work processes. This is a harsh judgment and one that many proponents of automation would challenge. But most automation efforts have simply accepted current processes and attempted to change how quickly work could be done—or reduce its labor-intensive content.

### Focus of Change/Key Assumption

Reengineering has the radical redesign of work processes as its central focus. Automation attempts to speed up the status quo and to seek cost reduction. Reengineering seeks the "creative destruction" of current processes. Automation sees its main objective as addressing the inefficient use of data.

### Output/Input Goal

Both approaches hold out the potential for performance improvement, but only reengineering seeks to achieve this while simultaneously reducing the demand for resources. Automation does not seek resource reduction as a normal course of action.

### Scope/Primary Target

The broad cross-functional scope of reengineering is quite different from automation, which often focuses on a specific activity such as order processing or financial transactions. Automation's target is improved data management. Reengineering seeks a new relationship with customers.

### Key Enabler

Both approaches use information technology as a key enabler. However, change management is considered a second essential enabler in reengineering, and it is most visible during the implementation stage of redesign.

## Duration

The life cycle of automation can sometimes be quite astounding. Some organizations spend many years attempting to change their technology. Reengineering can produce measurable benefits within a single year.

## Direction

The top-down direction for reengineering rarely occurs for automation. Instead, one typically finds that its support comes from the middle of the organization.

## Risk

With some notable exceptions (e.g., insurance) most businesses consider automation a moderate risk—certainly more moderate than the changes resulting from reengineering the core processes of the organization.

## Infrastructure Change

The demands in this area are substantial in reengineering. Automation requires more moderate change, such as reassignments based on eliminating labor-intensive tasks and, of course, the continued maintenance of systems installed.

## Improvement Goal

Because automation can extend the life of outmoded processes, one is tempted to say it actually results in a decrease in performance—mostly by making dumb things happen faster. To be charitable, one can say that the jury is out on automation. By contrast, we have seen that reengineering has the potential for, and has demonstrated, dramatic rates of improvement.

The distinction between automation and information technology is important. Automation is how technical change is applied; information technology is a means of changing how information is used. In short, automation is a decision; information technology is a tool. Reengineering deliberately embeds information technology within the team-based redesign effort and recognizes the need to do this very early in the design process.

## STAIRWAY TO HEAVEN

For many in the health care industry, reengineering will appear as competing with their current quality efforts. This is not a particularly accurate portrayal of the situation. Rather, as is shown in Figure 3.1, one should view both as having a legitimate and important role to play in any organization's improvement effort. It is important to match the approach to the situation. The choice of one over the other should reflect market pressures rather than personal preferences. As pointed out earlier, a quality program makes certain assumptions that may not reflect the reality facing the organization.

Faced with a longer time frame and a magnitude of change that does not require a radical departure from current processes, a TQM/CQI approach is quite sensible. Not only that, it offers a less disruptive transition to a new level of performance. However, for an organization needing to redesign its core processes within a fairly short period of time, reengineering is a more defensible choice. It is more disruptive and will certainly result in more political crosswinds, but it offers an opportunity for a quantum leap in performance. Unlike quality programs, its tools and techniques are not focused exclusively on maintaining equilibrium.

So, why not just reengineer all the time? Because it would simply burn out the organization. Trauma cannot be maintained without doing serious damage in the long run. Why not use TQM/CQI all the time? Because the market won't wait. By the time the organization reaches its desired performance level, it no longer offers a competitive advantage. Further, it would not benefit from a major redesign of the processes themselves. Finally, even those who

**Figure 3.1**  The Relationship between Reengineering and Quality Approaches

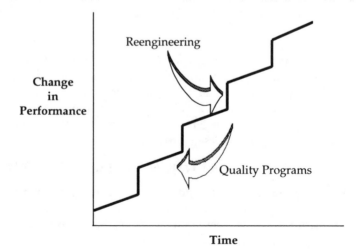

continue to adhere to the application of a continuous improvement model during these turbulent times concede a major issue exists.[6] As Figure 3.2 shows, a significant gap exists between the claims of proponents of quality programs and what has actually been delivered. Considering the pressure on health care organizations today, few can afford to wait to the length of time displayed in Figure 3.2 before significant improvements in performance are realized.

*Why not use TQM/CQI all the time? Because the market won't wait.*

Successful reengineering requires linking these two approaches together. To sustain the dramatic jump in performance requires the support of a continuous improvement approach. Fortunately, reengineering can "buy" the time required to pursue this, and organizations that have already pursued quality programs will find that their environments will be more supportive of a reengineering effort.

The motives for choosing reengineering vary. Just as quality is a "fix" for some and a "philosophy" for others, reengineering also can

**Figure 3.2** Barriers and Strategies for Staying on Track

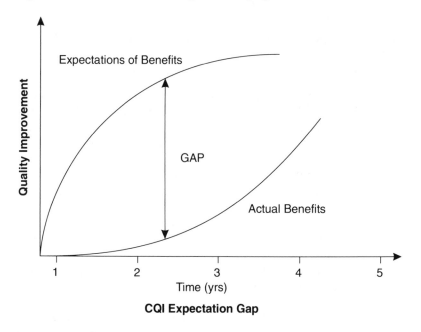

**CQI Expectation Gap**

© *Henry Ford Health System.*
*Reprinted with permission from Henry Ford Health System, as it appeared in* Reengineering Health Care: Building on CQI, *by J. R. Griffith, V. K. Sahney, and R. A. Mohr. Ann Arbor, MI: Health Administration Press, 1995.*

serve very different objectives. Some organizations are in serious trouble and turn to reengineering as a form of salvation—generally when it's too late. About half of the reengineering efforts occur because the organization perceives that a "threat" is on its way. A relatively small number of businesses recognize that reengineering can actually result in erecting a barrier to competition. These organizations may be among the first to recognize the value of establishing a vision and using time as a basis for developing a key capability.

## THE REENGINEERING PAYOFF

Organizations that achieve dramatic performance improvement pay particularly close attention to the key dimensions of reengineering: leadership, workforce, structure, and process. Our review of improvements brought about through reengineering begins with businesses outside the health care industry and then focuses on several within it.[7]

### British Airways

Achievements:

- Increased profits to $435 million, from a $900 million loss
- Increased passenger load by 16 percent.

When the British government decided to privatize its national airline in the mid-1980s, it turned to Colin Marshall to lead the effort. As an outsider, he faced a daunting task. His senior executive team had been drawn from the post-war Royal Air Force, and the organizational structure and culture emulated a military environment (staff continued to wear uniforms, for example). Top management believed a strong competitive advantage would come from building the best-engineered aircraft in the air.

The rigid segmentation of the organization's functions and the relative of regard for meeting customer preferences led to a growing loss of revenue. In fact, critics said the airline's initials stood for "bloody awful." Competition with other European airlines increased dramatically, so Marshall confronted his top team with this trend.

They insisted that the solution was to begin an advertising campaign to highlight how well their planes were engineered. Marshall countered by saying the problem was that people were unwilling to get inside them! After considerable debate, he took the dramatic step of firing nearly all of the top team and created a change effort called "Putting Customers First." The entire customer service process, from check-in to in-flight service, was redesigned. All British Airways employees received training and recognition to support a radical shift in customer service. Today British Airways is a preferred carrier among its domestic and international passengers.

## Citicorp

Achievements:

- Reported profits of $722 million after a loss of $914 million
- Reduced operating expenses by 12 percent.

Faced with a period of losses, write-offs due to bad real estate loans, and the close watch of bank examiners, Citicorp's CEO, John Reed, introduced sweeping changes in the bank's processes and culture in the early 1990s that required him to make personal changes as well. He had long promoted the value of decentralized management and strategic thinking. However, he recognized that it would be necessary for him to play a far more hands-on role to ensure the success of this change, so he began to attend to a level of detail that previously had been left to others. By changing the way Citicorp processed products and data, Reed sought to reach a target of $1 billion in cost reduction. He made no secret of his assessment of his top management team. One of his most recent moves was to hire Christopher Steffen, the former Kodak CFO who left after only 11 weeks due to differences with the Kodak CEO over how quickly it should sell assets and cut costs. Steffen's arrival at Citicorp is seen as a step toward enhancing Citicorp's management talent.

## Motorola

Achievements:

- Reduced in-process defect levels 150 times in five years
- Saves $2.2 billion in manufacturing costs.

The name Motorola used to be associated with television sets. Recognizing the radical shift in the electronics market, Robert Galvin, the CEO, decided in the early 1990s to sell Motorola's Quasar brand to Matsushita Electrical Industrial Company of Japan and focus solely on microchips and wireless devices. The immediate industry reaction was that this was just another example of an American company throwing in the towel in its failed attempt to compete with the Japanese. However, Galvin recognized that

Motorola's current processes were unable to achieve the level of performance that would put the company in a lead market. He set dramatic performance targets that included reducing manufacturing defects by 90 percent every two years and cycle time by 90 percent every five years. The internal culture also changed, and it now emphasizes the anticipation of change and the creative potential in dissent and open "verbal combat." Today, Motorola is the world's leader in producing wireless devices. Its recent joint effort with IBM and Apple to produce the PowerPC microprocessor has positioned it as a challenger in this market as well.

## Hallmark

Achievements:

- Reduced product development cycle to less than a year
- Improved quality of product designs.

It is hard for most of us to imagine just how competitive the greeting card market has become. In the early '90s, Robert Stack, Hallmark's CEO, recognized a consumer move toward specialty items and diverse channels of distribution. Although not generally acknowledged, Hallmark also saw the potential for losing a substantial share of its market to competitors who were gaining access to mass retailers. The processes that led Hallmark to develop products faster than it could sell them were subject to a radical redesign. The primary targets were to reduce cycle time and reduce cost. To set the stage for their reengineering effort, the senior team spent considerable effort creating a future view for Hallmark and agreed on a set of core values and beliefs that would guide the organization and its people.

## University of Virginia Medical Center

Achievements:

- Reduction in administrative costs
- Accelerated billing
- Reduced accounts receivable days
- Increased cash flow.

The primary focus of most health care organizations today is on cost. The University of Virginia Medical Center in Charlottesville employs over 4,000 people and has payroll costs in excess of $11.5 million. Their reengineering effort of the early '90s focused on four major electronic communication projects: the use of optical character recognition to automate patient billing; the ability to accept electronic remittance advice from Medicare fiscal intermediaries; on-line preadmission eligibility checks; and automated procedures to post collection agency payments.

## Other Hospital Efforts

Many hospitals are seeking to reduce inventory, increase productivity, reduce processing time, and improve quality through their reengineering efforts. Three hospitals located in Arizona, Minnesota, and southern California focused on turning receivables into cash quickly and efficiently. The results of their process redesign are quite impressive. These three hospitals have reduced their days in accounts receivable from 208 to 104, from 88 to 55, and from 110 to 63, respectively.

## Connecticut Mutual Life

Achievements:

- Productivity gain of 60 percent
- Improved customer service.

Many insurance companies were surprised to hear themselves described as "paper factories" just a few years ago. The comparison to manufacturing, however, offered an opportunity to adopt improvement approaches from the manufacturing industry. Indeed, the realization that it had a paper-driven, clerical-based, factory-like work flow is what led Connecticut Mutual Life to turn to reengineering at the beginning of this decade. Their reengineering effort involved the installation of imaging technology combined with work flow software to capture, store, retrieve, and route paper-based information. Their redesign team's concept was to allow several people to work on a single document at the same time. Thus, a sequential process was turned into a simultaneous and parallel one. The use of technology as an enabler also helped reduce a significant amount of tedious work, allowing employees to spend less time on paper processing and more on serving clients.

## Mutual Benefit Life

Achievements

- Halved the cost of the issuance and underwriting process.

Faced with a declining real estate portfolio, Henry Kates, the CEO of Mutual Benefit Life, decided to pursue reengineering in the early 1990s to help streamline business processes and reduce cost. The goal was to save $1 million out of a $7 million budget. The processes that offered the most significant opportunity for redesign were the issuance of policies and the underwriting process.

## Aetna

Achievements:

- Reduced number of claims inquiries
- Savings of $700 million through redesigned enrollment process.

Ron Compton, CEO of Aetna, has gained a reputation in the insurance industry for being an outspoken critic of bureaucracy. After reviewing Aetna's processes and culture in the early 1990s, he concluded that customers were often regarded as an intrusion in the working day. He has pursued a course of reorganizing three divisions into 15 new strategic business units (SBUs), each with demanding performance targets. Some of the main reengineering activities included reuniting personal and commercial lines of property and casualty insurance, piloting image-processing technology to handle claims, and introducing the use of laptop computers at customer sites to enroll prospective members and print out their identification cards instantly.

## Blue Cross Blue Shield of Washington/Alaska

Achievements:

- Increased electronic claims submission from 11 to 30 percent
- Decreased operating cost ratio from 13.6 to 10 percent
- Increased market share from 14 to 18 percent.

The market facing Blue Cross Blue Shield of Washington/Alaska (BCWA) has become one of the most competitive in the nation. In 1989, BCWA had an operating cost ratio of 13.6 percent, a measure of total administrative costs as a proportion of revenues. Betty Woods, the CEO, set a target of 7 percent by 1995. In 1992 fewer than 11 percent of BCWA's claims were received electronically. Although it took ten days to handle a claim, only 5.2 minutes of actual work time was involved—the remaining time was consumed by an inefficient process. The reengineering effort began by seeking "quick hits" to reduce cost. Between 1992 and 1993, BCWA achieved administrative savings in excess of $3 million; their goal is $18 million per year by 1995.

## Emory Clinic

Achievements:

- Patients move through radiology at faster pace
- Patients' return time to orthopedics down 40 percent.

Reengineering seeks ways to reduce inefficiency by improving cooperation between functional areas. At the Emory Clinic in Atlanta, the target of such an effort was the relationship between the orthopedics and radiology departments. Traditionally, when an orthopedic surgeon at the clinic decided an x-ray was needed, the patient was sent over to radiology. Because no appointment had been made, the patient usually had a significant wait. The orthopedics department reengineered this process in conjunction with radiology, and developed an information exchange that allowed orthopedics to schedule appointments via computer.

## Mercy Hospital

Achievements:

- Reduced infection rates
- Decrease in lab work cycle time
- Increased patient satisfaction
- Reduced lab errors.

Mercy Hospital, located in San Diego, found itself in an increasingly competitive market—a description many in southern California would regard as an understatement! An assessment of its processes found that small organizational units had largely unpredictable workloads that resulted in considerable idle time. It was difficult to handle these swings because the hospital's highly specialized staff had limited flexibility in scheduling. In addition, any savings that could be achieved were overshadowed by the cost of coordinating, scheduling, documenting, and managing highly inefficient care processes. Their reengineering effort, referred to as "Care 2000," called for placing of services closer to patients, simplifying processes, and expanding the qualifications and skills of care providers.

## Sentara Health System

Achievements:

- Reduced diagnostic radiology time
- Cut costs in major procedures
- Decreased numbers of infections and medication errors
- Increased employee satisfaction.

In 1989, Sentara, located in Norfolk, Virginia, found that 30 to 40 percent of their time spent on inpatient care was not productive. By 1990 they decided to address these issues through a continuous quality improvement effort and found that the problems were related to scheduling, documenting, duplication of effort, and overspecialization among certain positions.

Although Sentara improved, it needed to become even more aggressive. Finally, they adopted a reengineering approach, which was driven by David Bernd, their executive vice president and chief operating officer. Sentara has successfully combined its quality improvement and reengineering efforts.

Sentara found that its cumbersome admissions process contained 47 steps and resulted in a 90-minute delay in most cases. They streamlined this process, and it now requires only 17 steps and takes five to ten minutes to complete. Sentara has used a patient-focused hospital concept to guide its efforts, and its results are quite impressive. Their diagnostics radiology turnaround time from order entry to film processing has been reduced from 391 minutes to 68 minutes. The costs for DRG 148—major small and large bowel procedures—were reduced by 13.3 percent. Postoperative wound infections decreased by 33 percent, urinary tract infections fell by 12 percent, medication errors were reduced 50 percent, and patient satisfaction increased from a range of 85 to 95 percent to a range of 95 to 100 percent.

## Matthew Thornton Health Care

Achievements:

- One of the highest profitability and liquidity ratios of all HMOs in the United States
- Came in first in a recent nationwide customer satisfaction survey
- Increased marketshare.

This is a relatively small group-model HMO, located in New Hampshire, with approximately 107,000 members. In the 1990–1991 period, the company was losing more than 300 members a month and had not introduced a new product in over 20 years. After spending over a year developing a point-of-service product, only 200 of its current 63,000 members were willing to sign up. The product, created by actuaries, underwriters, and operational representatives, was designed to be easy for the company to administer but forced those using it back into the HMO network—the illusion of choice.[8]

The company decided a dramatic shift in thinking was needed and began a reengineering effort in 1992. It formed a small team that represented a cross-functional view of the organization. Working on a part-time basis, the team identified five core processes: service and education; medical care management; developing quality provider networks; claims processing and payment; and customer acquisition.

To address the process of developing quality provider networks, it changed its pay scheme with its affiliated physicians to be one that offered a fixed monthly amount for managing each patient and discounted payments for the services provided. The cost and quality of the treatment was taken into account for purposes of calculating the amount of payment for each patient. Within seven months, it had more affiliated physicians than its competitors.

The process of medical care management benefited from a page from reengineering completed in other industries. There it is found that skimping on input means extra effort and resources required for rework, rejects, and returns. A medical care equivalent was found in caring for premature infants. Mothers showing signs of potential premature labor were treated and sent home after the symptoms stopped. The cost of two more days of hospitalization to minimize the risk of actual premature delivery would be approximately $5,000. They found that one in 20 cases with potential premature delivery actually resulted in a premature birth. Treatment costs for the infant would be about $500,000. It was decided that spending $100,000 to cover the 20 cases would result in avoiding the $500,000 for treatment. Until there was more attention spent on outcomes instead of symptoms, such options would never be considered.

## IT'S ALWAYS SOMETHING · · · · · · · · · · ·

As impressive as these health care reengineering results are, those involved would be the first to say that much remains to be done. Many are still trying to work out the relationship between quality improvement and reengineering. Others know they need a tighter link to their organization's strategy. Many of the examples cited here are still a considerable distance from achieving the organizationwide change they need. In fact, some would not hold up to close scrutiny by anyone applying a rigid definition of reengineering. Still, they are clearly heading in the right direction, and their early successes have won them support for further effort.

*Those involved would be the first to say that much remains to be done.*

Nearly all have had some humbling experiences in the implementation stage. You can fake a lot of stuff—but not that. In

Chapter 5 we will return to a discussion of health care processes and revisit some of the reengineering insights that have been gained by these early pioneers.

## SUMMARY

Reengineering is a relatively new approach in the health care industry. As such, it is important to understand how it compares to other approaches. In addition, it is important to keep a focus on the tangible benefits that can be achieved.

Although reengineering shares common ground with several other approaches, its differences are quite pronounced. Its scope, goals, targets, and potential for performance improvement help explain why it is gaining popularity in health care. Yet, such comparisons often mask an important issue that gets lost in the debate. Reengineering and the quality approaches are complementary, not adversaries. An organization can—and should—make use of both, but it needs to match each approach's capabilities with the magnitude and type of change required for the organization.

Many organizations have discovered that it is possible to achieve dramatic performance improvements through the application of reengineering. Although health care reengineering efforts are still in their early stages, their outcomes have been impressive. Hospitals, insurers, and many others are finding that it is possible to achieve significant change by managing the four key dimensions—leadership, workforce, structure, and process— within a reengineering effort.

Clearly, more has to be done. The full potential of reengineering cannot be reached without a better understanding of how an organization can support it and how to use teams to pursue radical process redesign. Chapter 4 will look more closely at these issues.

### Notes

1. Frankly, I feel that these comparisons, while necessary, are a thankless task. There is little hope of changing the minds of the zealots who push their preferred approaches. Further, it is fully expected that these comparisons will be regarded as either prejudicial or weak by one side or the other. People who are responsible for creating business forecasts will empathize with this predicament. On the other hand, the comparisons do offer the opportunity for debate. I have tried to draw as carefully as I can from the literature and my own experiences as I tread this treacherous path.

2. Articles and books exploring alternatives to reengineering are listed in the bibliography at the end of this book.

3. TQM and employee involvement are compared in E. E. Lawler III, 1994, "Total Quality Management and Employee Involvement:

Are They Compatible?" *Academy of Management Executive* 8 (1): 68–76. I am also struck by the similarities between employee involvement and reengineering, particularly with regard to the degree of autonomy required by people within teams in order to achieve breakthrough thinking. I am sure that the next time I see Lawler, he will point out that I am not doing justice to employee involvement.

4. It continues to amaze me how often one finds this type of characterization. For example, in R. W. Keidel, 1994, "Rethinking Organization Design," *The Academy of Management Executive* 8 (November): 12–30, the author states that restructuring (which he uses as a category that includes downsizing) only differs from reengineering in degree. His preferred approach, "rethinking," shares characteristics found frequently in the reengineering literature. I have seen "rethinking" as a key component of several reengineering efforts in health care.

5. See W. E. Halal, 1994, "From Hierarchy to Enterprise: Internal Markets Are the New Foundation of Management," *The Academy of Management Executive* 8 (November): 69–83. Halal offers an insightful overview of another negative outcome from downsizing— particularly among middle management. His position is that the strategic role of middle management is often overlooked and that individuals whose roles have provided them with knowledge that can help an organization identify and develop key capabilities will be lost if the organization does not recognize distinctions between tactical and strategic middle-management positions as they seek to "delayer."

6. For additional discussion on the CQI expectation gap, see J. R. Griffith, V. K. Sahney, and R. A. Mohr, 1995, *Reengineering Health Care: Building on CQI* (Ann Arbor, MI: Health Administration Press), 286–87.

7. The bibliography at the end of this book lists references on the reengineering efforts at British Airways, Citicorp, Motorola, and Hallmark, as well as on the health care reengineering examples.

8. Unfortunately, organizations too often wind up elbowing their way to the head of the line. I was particularly impressed with a recent discussion of this in J. Champy, 1995, *Reengineering Management* (New York: Harper Business).

## CHAPTER 4

# Reengineering the Business through Process Reengineering

*We are much better than anyone else who doesn't know what they are doing.*

A reengineering leadership group

**A** TTEMPTING REENGINEERING on a limited scale is like seeking battlefield advantage with a small nuclear device. Either one will result in new meaning to the phrase "mission creep." The point is that reengineering is an approach designed to effect large-scale organizational change. As such, it requires careful positioning and support to ensure success. In this chapter, we will look at the organizational activity that surrounds reengineering, including the formation of redesign teams and the work they do.

Of particular importance here is the distinction between *business reengineering* and *process reengineering*. The former refers to what an organization must do to wrap itself around the actual redesign of core processes and business processes. The latter defines the actual work done to achieve the redesign of these processes. This chapter will provide an overview of both and their relationship to each other. It will show why successful reengineering includes and must also go beyond process redesign.

## WHAT'S NEW?

When people first began to hear about reengineering, it struck many as either too mechanistic or something that pertained solely to changing the flow of work—process redesign. As Figure 4.1 portrays, the reality is quite different. The arrival of new processes leads to new jobs. New jobs lead to a wide array of changes required to ensure that the new jobs are performed in the way that the new process intended. Focusing on process design, to the exclusion of these other issues, will blunt the full potential of reengineering.

We can expect, for example, that the current organization simply does not have people with the skills required to do the new jobs. Of course, one way to deal with this is through the acquisition of knowledge or experience via training or job rotation. But eventually the organization will have to bring in people with the needed attributes. The shift from a vertical to a horizontal structure will result in the loss of old career paths and the emergence of new ones.

The glue that keeps all this together is organizational infrastructure—new values that guide the direction of work and the relationships that surround it and new forms of compensation, particularly in organizations where team-based efforts are required to carry out the redesigned processes. In sum, any organization that comes to appreciate the "ripple effect" that process change causes can be forgiven for being taken aback by their daunting task. Reengineering is a major challenge and one that requires significant planning and managing. An organization must understand how to "wrap" itself around a reengineering effort.

*An organization must understand how to "wrap" itself around a reengineering effort.*

## BUSINESS REENGINEERING

The organizational effort to initiate, guide, and support a health care reengineering effort is called *business reengineering*, and it is defined as follows:

**Figure 4.1**  The Inevitable Outcome of Process Redesign

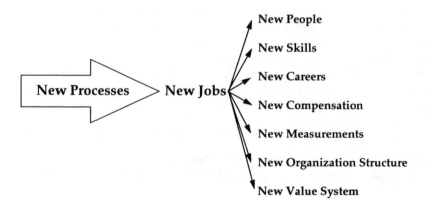

*The alignment of reengineered core processes with organiza-
tional infrastructure to achieve key capabilities that deliver
outcomes valued by customers.*

Clearly, we are calling for a major transformation of a business,
not just a transactional change on a lesser scale. As the definition
implies, it is necessary to go beyond process redesign if one
is to achieve the dramatic jump in performance expected from
reengineering.[1] More specifically, business reengineering has the
following objectives:

- Radical design/redesign of business processes
- Realigned organizational infrastructure
- New policies, management, and measurement systems
- Breaking rules through the use of information technol-
  ogy
- New working environment
- Revised mix of skills
- Sustained performance through continuous improve-
  ment.

These objectives begin with the pursuit of radical process change.
(We refer to this later as process reengineering because it describes
the work done by teams focused on core processes and the
business processes within them.) The rest of the list describes
the transformation of an entire organization, as a direct result of
the reengineering effort.

## A BUSINESS REENGINEERING MODEL

Figure 4.2 presents a conceptual model for business reengineering.
The physical appearance of this model is meant to convey the
specific components of business reengineering. The first box sets
the stage by identifying the scope of the reengineering effort itself.
This is followed by establishing an organizational entity specifically
designed to govern the reengineering effort, coupled with the
selection of teams charged with the process redesign work.

The center boxes of the model show three strands of activity
taking place simultaneously. The enabling power of information
technology and the alignment of organizational infrastructure
parallel the actual redesign (or reengineering) of processes. This
tight linkage is critical for achieving optimal reengineering results.

The need to coordinate implementation is tied to continuous
improvement, an explicit acknowledgment of the relationship
between reengineering and quality management. Finally, we see
that the entire effort rests on management of change, which is
viewed by reengineering experts as a critical ingredient for success.

**Figure 4.2**  A Business Reengineering Model

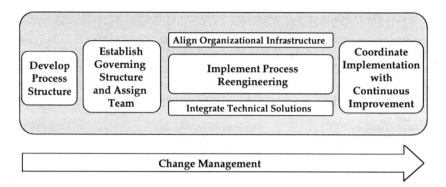

Business reengineering requires that specific goals are accomplished in each of these areas. We now focus on each of the model's components.

## Develop Process Structure

The senior executive team in a health care business bears responsibility for setting the organization's strategy. For some, this is a tedious and somewhat mechanical process that does little more than create goals and objectives that are subsequently subdivided and redefined to guide the work within existing functions. The business reengineering model calls for a series of crucial activities that establish the direction for the entire reengineering effort. These activities include establishing the corporate direction, agreeing on reengineering as the approach to pursue, identifying what we call the "two C's" (capabilities and core processes), approving a governing structure, and allocating resources.

### Corporate Direction

Top management must ensure that reengineering is linked to business strategy. Of course, this assumes that a vision and strategy, including a direction for information technology, have been developed. Corporate direction should include corporate objectives and values to guide the organization in the future. Reengineering simply cannot succeed without this business context, and it can only come from a deliberate choice to use this approach as the vehicle to move the organization in a new direction.

### Agree on Approach

Top management will face a critical decision when they assess the magnitude of change they need. At this moment, they will have to choose a change approach that meets their level of demand. The top team will need a working knowledge of the approaches available to them. Selecting an educational process to gain this knowledge is also important.

Many senior managers attempt to make such decisions without investigating the nuances of reengineering. They later find themselves annoyed and surprised to find out what they endorsed. Further, without taking the time to understand reengineering, they often fail to understand how critical their own roles are in ensuring success. Some of these roles are described below.

## Leadership

Even experienced executives face transitions of this magnitude only once or twice during their careers. Under these circumstances, the organization needs a strong, tenacious, and courageous person at the top who steps into the role of leader. Above all, this individual signals through the use of power and presence that reengineering is not only acceptable, it is essential and will not be deterred by other organizational events. With turnover common in key top-level positions, reengineering is often at risk of being abandoned upon the arrival of the new order. Thus, establishing reengineering leadership requires developing a broad base of support that can withstand such transitions.

## Transformation Climate

Top management must take steps to educate the organization about what is about to happen, to communicate their intentions, and to take an active role in meeting opposition. The climate must endorse the radical rethinking that reengineering requires and reward those who show a willingness to take a calculated risk. The climate will be shaped by what we call "social architecting," including the careful placement of champions.

## Position for Change

The visibility of top management is not only critical for people inside the business, it is also vital for customers, regulators, and other stakeholders. Top management must play a prominent role in explaining what they are doing to their business and what outcomes they expect. A strategic communication plan is the best vehicle to guide these executive efforts.

## Adhere to Priorities

As the potential for disruption from reengineering becomes apparent to the organization, resistance will mount steadily. Top management must be prepared to deal with this resistance.[2] In general, resistance comes in four forms: rationality, fear, discomfort, and skepticism. It surfaces from difference sources at different stages during a reengineering effort. (Resistance in health care settings will be discussed further in Chapter 7.)

During early direction sitting and diagnosis, skepticism and fear comes from everywhere. During redesign, resistance comes in the form of rejection and dismissal from middle management. During implementation, resistance shows up as noncompliance and defiance, often from the bottom of the organization and from senior managers. Because physicians generally outlast CEOs, they are the players most likely to make or break reengineering efforts. One of the more common reengineering mistakes is for top management to "pull the plug" at the first sign of trouble. Turbulence is to be expected.

## The "Two C's"

Our reengineering overview presented a staircase with critical steps for top management to take. The "Two C's" pertain to top management's identification of the key capabilities and core processes. The subsequent work done by process teams is highly dependent on this being accomplished and agreed to by senior management.

The health care industry poses a substantial challenge for a top executive team attempting to meet this objective. In Chapter 5 we will return to this issue because it is important to gain some idea of what these capabilities and processes might look like in health care.

## Governing Structure

In any large-scale change effort, senior managers must accept their roles and responsibilities, and then move on to create a governing structure to oversee the reengineering effort. They must decide who they will assign as the core process owners. "Governance" here is not the equivalent of what one expects from a board of trustees. The governing structure consists of those with operational accountability for the organization, and it is constructed specifically to oversee the reengineering effort. This body can be—and probably should be—directly accountable to the CEO or the board of trustees. Without their support, it may be impossible to gain support for the radical redesign implications that are likely to surface.

Neglecting to create an organizational body made up of people with the stature, knowledge, and accountability for overseeing a reengineering effort would be a fatal mistake—like acquiring the world's most expensive toaster and having no place to plug it in. We will discuss the governing body in more detail in the next section.

## Allocate Resources

One of the most contentious points in getting started is the choice of key people to become process team members. Top management must agree on who will be made available and for how long. Process owners are highly dependent on this support. Later we will look at team selection criteria.

### Establish Governing Structure and Assign Team

A health care organization intending to pursue reengineering will need to create a fairly robust structure that will oversee the reengineering effort.[3] Some people may think that this is just another steering committee, but steering committees are often not strong enough to handle this assignment. Their members are not necessarily senior-level managers. Even senior managers tend to view their presence on steering committees as "showing the flag" more than actually providing direction. Finally, steering committee members often have too little "skin in the game" and delegate decision making when difficult issues arise.

Figure 4.3 shows the key positions in a governing structure: those who lead the reengineering effort, owners of the processes to be redesigned, a "reengineering czar," the process teams, and a pool of resources to support the teams. This figure also shows the organizational relationships among the key governing structure positions. The process owner(s) and the reengineering czar having a direct reporting relationship to the reengineering leadership group at the top of the organization. The dotted-line relationship between the czar and the process owner(s) indicates that the czar provides support to the process owners—an area we will discuss in more detail later.

The process owner has a direct connection to a process team that will be redesigning a core process. The teams are supported by a resource pool under the direction of the reengineering czar. The selection of these players and the management of this governing structure constitutes one of the most demanding aspects of business reengineering. Frankly, organizations that give this insufficient attention are those who have been supplying the literature with recent examples of failures. To avoid this in the health care industry, we offer the following discussion of the organizational relationships among these positions, what each

**Figure 4.3**  Business Reengineering Governing Structure

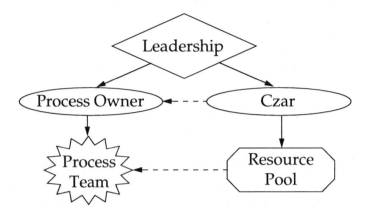

contributes, and how this fits within the concept of business reengineering.

## Reengineering Leadership

The success of a reengineering effort is determined by the degree to which top executives understand and fulfill a leadership role. The primary activities within this role are the following:

- **Select process owners**: The leadership group is most likely a subset of the top management team. Having completed their earlier responsibilities we have mentioned regarding setting the stage for reengineering, they now assume a reengineering leadership role and begin by selecting process owners. We will discuss the characteristics of these individuals later.

- **Make decisions**: Throughout the reengineering effort, process owners and perhaps representatives of the process teams will be coming to the leadership group for a review of their effort and to request approval to move forward. This requires the leadership group to be informed of the activity and aware of the potential impact their decisions will have on other parts of the organization.

- **Monitor progress**: One of the key elements associated with successful reengineering is the setting of aggressive measures of success. This group is accountable for seeing that the reengineering effort will help the organization achieve these goals. To that end, this group must examine the progress of the process teams and identify, address, and resolve any deviation from planned activity.

- **Integrate/support effort**: To ensure that multiple reengineering efforts are carried out in an orchestrated manner, the leadership group must work closely with the process owners to help them make optimal use of the committed resources and to keep the multiple efforts from impeding one another. Reengineering leaders also make certain that process owners and teams have adequate support from the rest of the organization. This includes the systems applications and infrastructure alignment needed to support the organizationwide impact of process redesign.

## Process Owners

In Chapter 2 we discussed the lack of process accountability found within most organizations. To begin to address this, someone must be given the authority and responsibility for seeing that a selected core process is redesigned. The role of the process owner is a critical reengineering role requiring the following characteristics:

- **Experience and innovation**: One of the primary considerations for choosing a process owner is that he or she must have had sufficient experience within some of the key areas of the business that will be affected by reengineering. This experience, however, needs to be coupled with a reputation for being a respected manager, particularly among peers. The process owner should be someone who has demonstrated innovative thinking and a willingness to take on difficult assignments in a manner that encourages the support of others. Process owners report to the reengineering leadership group.

    *If you think the business may suffer if you appoint an individual to the team, that person belongs on the team.*

- **Authority**: Because reengineering focuses on horizontal cross-functional business processes, the process owner must be given the authority to address these relationships and take the necessary steps to radically redesign how they will operate in the future. Granting this authority is one of the most difficult tasks for an organization because it runs counter to the current power structure and political influence system.

- **Process team selection**: The process owner is given the authority to request key people from across the organization to become members of his or her process team. It is worth noting that the relationship this person has to the team is not necessarily one of providing day-to-day direction. Rather, it is one of being the customer of the team, a customer with the responsibility for getting the work done. An early test of top executive support for the reengineering effort comes when there is resistance to the process owner's team selections. Some people say that if you think the business may suffer if you appoint an individual to the team, that person belongs on the team.

- **Career commitment**: In many respects, assuming the role of process owner is a "bet the farm" career move. Few assignments will have the visibility, accountability, and turbulence that this one does.[4] The person must be willing to give a minimum of 30 percent of his or her time to this work. The outcome of this person's assigned responsibility could very well decide the future success or failure of the organization.

## Process Teams

The "engine" in reengineering is the process team. The selection and preparation of these teams are among the most important steps taken in a reengineering effort. This is because the choice of people to carry out this work will determine the degree of innovation and insightful change achieved. These teams generally constitute about ten people and combine a mixture of skills and experiences that form a powerful opportunity for process redesign. Reporting relationships vary, but they range from self-directed, to having a team captain, to a direct relationship to the process owner. Key characteristics of these teams include the following:

*The "engine" in reengineering is the process team.*

- **Cross-functional**: Three to five members of the team should be chosen on the basis of their knowledge of the processes to be redesigned. They bring an understanding of the business and its customers, and certain skills that will contribute to a team-based effort: communication, interpersonal, analytical, and diagnostic.

- **Multidisciplinary**: The most successful reengineering teams bring a diverse set of skills to bear on their work. About two to three members often bring general business knowledge and an understanding of the culture. Some of these individuals are experts in current functional areas, and others bring expertise in support areas such as information technology, organization change, reengineering, human resources, and finance.

- **The "radical few"**: The worst characteristic of a team is homogeneity. In fact, it is precisely the opposite that tends to encourage innovation. You need one or two people who represent the "yeast" within the team. They can be outside consultants or insiders who can "think out of the box" when called upon. They are the organizational mavericks who live their careers on the margin of social acceptability—unreasonable people who won't accept the status quo.

- **The Vikings**: There is no agreement on the level of effort required by a reengineering team. Some people believe that members should be dedicated full-time for at least a year—or until the implementation begins. Others find that they can achieve results with less of a time demand. This is a very difficult decision and one for which there is no hard and fast rule. The guiding principle, however, is that a reengineering effort should be of prime importance to the future of the organization. Any decision to allow less than full-time participation should weigh the potential for suboptimal results against the loss of these individuals for this period.

  Another key area for debate concerns the future role of these team members. Remember the point about how the Vikings burned their ships upon arrival? Team members should not plan to return to their previous positions. Their new "home" will be made in the environment and processes they create. Otherwise, the organization runs the risk of decisions being made that are not subject to their reality check.

## Reengineering Czar

The role of reengineering czar is an interesting one, partly because the role requires an in-depth understanding of reengineering and the organization, and partly because of the nature of the reporting relationships between this position and others. Political skills are paramount, as the characteristics described below make clear:

- **Supporting the process owner**: This individual is the "keeper of the faith" in terms of the methodology and tools. There is a need to maintain a balance between innovation and adherence to reengineering principles. Overall, this person is held accountable for ensuring that the reengineering approach selected by the organization is followed as intended. The czar has a dual reporting relationship—to the leadership group and to the process owners.

- **Resource allocation:** The czar is often given a resource pool to draw from in supporting the work of the process design teams. In addition to internal talent, this pool may contain outside consultants who bring expertise not otherwise available to the organization. This expertise often includes reengineering knowledge, management of large-scale change, and information technology. It is up to the czar to ensure the availability of these resources to the process teams.

- **Corporate liaison/advisor:** The reengineering czar serves a key advisory role to the reengineering leadership group and as a reengineering process advisor to the process owners. As such, he or she is in a position to monitor the progress being made and how the reengineering resources are being used. The most important part of this responsibility is ensuring that multiple reengineering efforts are receiving adequate support and identifying issues that would prevent this.

- **Communication/training:** It is important that the czar sees to it that the people involved in reengineering work are prepared to carry out their roles and that the rest of the organization receives appropriate communication about their effort. This may require cooperation with organizational areas that are responsible for communication and training, but it can also be treated as a separate responsibility. It is imperative that the training include the education of top management.

Some have asked why the CEO and COO are not likely to be the best choices to play the role of the czar. First, the CEO may be consumed with external relationships, particularly at a time when top executives are constantly involved in negotiating mergers and other political and financial matters. By definition, the role of the CEO is to pay more attention to external than internal matters. Why then doesn't the COO fill the role of the czar? The primary reason is that the demands of the position simply do not allow for the time required to fill the duties described above *and* the normal responsibilities of the job.

## Resource Pool

Health care organizations often find that it is impossible to free up enough staff to participate in a reengineering effort. Under these circumstances, a pool of people can be created to augment the teams. This is a delicate issue, however. There needs to be sufficient internal ownership of the team effort or the implementation process is likely to be rejected by the organization. Before establishing such a pool, the following considerations are important:

- **The "odd couple"**: Reengineering draws upon an unusual mix of information technology and organization change expertise from individuals deliberately paired and pre-pared to help support the work done by process teams. This is a particularly difficult blend to manage, and there is a natural tendency to drift toward one's "comfort zone." The integration of these skill sets probably will not happen without the czar's influence.

- **Reengineering consultants**: Some individuals within this pool will become process team members. In this capacity, they offer guidance on the enabling power of information technology in support of process redesign options. They also advise the teams on the application of reengineering tools and techniques. Others in the pool become "behind the scenes" experts in the design of tools, methodology, or systems applications that support the process teams. Thus, the teams include people from the resource pool who are direct contributors and their "extended family."

- **Communication/training**: Individuals in the pool are of-ten specially chosen and prepared to offer communication and training to the corporation as well as the process teams. The extent of their accountability is determined by the capability elsewhere in the organization. They might advise, design, or deliver these services.

- **Prototype design/support**: An often overlooked source of expertise within the pool are individuals with the experience and knowledge needed to create a model office or some prototype environment to determine the feasibility of chosen process designs. This requires a blend of information technology, work design, and physical environment layout.

## Align the Organizational Infrastructure

We have discussed the need to develop a process structure, create a governing structure, and assign process teams. Returning to our business reengineering model, we see three boxes in the center. Activities in these boxes are carried out simultaneously. We begin with a discussion of the first, *align the organizational infrastructure.*

A "personnel handbook" is a documented record of organizational failures that led to bureaucratization in the form of policy.

The phrase "organizational infrastructure" may strike you as somewhat odd. We don't often think about all the things around us that support our work and reinforce our behavior on a daily basis. Just as we don't generally spend much time staring at the underside of bridges, we don't pay much attention to the support systems in our organizations. Ironically, these systems determine whether a redesigned process will succeed or fail.[5] A further irony is that many organizations find it harder to make infrastructure changes than to redesign processes. To understand this, we examine how reengineering relies on the alignment of the organizational infrastructure.

## Skills Mix

Reengineering poses a major challenge for many organizations because they are faced with the reality that dramatic changes in process will require performance beyond the capability of their current workforce. If time permits and a sufficient degree of talent exists, internal training and development may meet these needs. Otherwise, they will have to revise the criteria and process used to bring new talent into the organization. In either case, this aspect of the current infrastructure will undergo major change.

## Policy Shifts

A "personnel handbook" is a documented record of organizational failures that led to bureaucratization in the form of policy. These policies often lie dormant until process teams begin proposing changes in working conditions, changes that will be impeded by current policies. A significant effort will have to be made to untangle the policy and procedure web that reengineering will encounter.

## Team-Based Support

One of the key issues that process change encounters is the shift in work design that calls for a team-based work environment. Most organizations have human resources systems that are not geared toward a team-based environment. Training, reward systems, performance measurements, and career growth will all be subject to review. A fundamental change in management behavior is needed to support a shift in power and accountability tied to process redesign.

## Psychological Contract

One of the most difficult decisions an organization ever has to make is to reduce its workforce because of process changes. It requires the establishment of "mechanical" procedures for doing so and draws attention to the underlying psychological contract between the organization and its employees. We will return to this issue in Chapter 7 when we discuss how change management is embedded within a reengineering effort.

## Implement Process Reengineering

To understand the essence of reengineering, it is necessary to focus on the work performed by process redesign teams. Recall that the team members are chosen by process owners and provided by the reengineering leadership. We refer to this work as *Process reengineering.*

### A Definition

The business reengineering model in Figure 4.2 includes a component labeled *Implement Process Reengineering.* It is defined as follows:

> *The fundamental and radical redesign of business processes to achieve dramatic organizational improvements in cost, quality, and access.*

The focus is on business processes. Why? The main reason is that it is impossible to redesign a core process without addressing the business processes within it. In health care, teams will seek performance improvements in the three central measures of the industry: cost, quality, and access. The objectives of process reengineering are like several we saw earlier in business reengineering. However, this time the work is being performed at a finer level of detail, such as the following:

- Radical design/redesign of business processes
- Proposed realignment of organizational infrastructure
- New process measurements
- Use of information technology as a process enabler
- Prototype new working environment
- Propose new skills mix
- Support process redesign through continuous improvement.

This list helps define the scope of work performed by the teams. They will seek radical design or redesign of processes and ensure that such changes can be implemented successfully. Before we look more closely at the work performed, let us first recall how these teams are formed.

Figure 4.4 shows the formation of a process team. The most obvious criterion for selecting teams relates to the nature of the core process to be redesigned. Team members must have sufficient knowledge and experience to help examine and redesign the business processes within the core process. Many of these people are likely to be drawn from the different functional areas that form the "path" for the core process. The remaining team members come from the resource pool under the direction of the reengineering czar. These players bring information technology insight and reengineering experience to the team.

The team now has its permanent members. Over time, they are likely to draw upon other individuals for advice and assistance. These may be people inside the organization who have knowledge or influence to help guide the team. In addition, customers often are sought out for insights and reactions to help the team decide on the direction of the process redesign.

The reengineering czar is responsible for preparing these teams to do their work. Generally, each team member is given training in the reengineering approach and an explanation of their roles, responsibilities, and how their effort relates to the governing structure. At this point they are ready to pursue process redesign.

## A Process Reengineering Model

Process reengineering is at the center of the business reengineering model and contains five steps: process direction, process diagnosis,

**Figure 4.4** Forming a Process Redesign Team

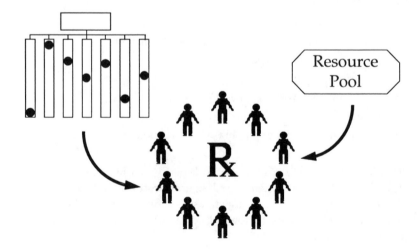

process fast-path, process redesign, and process implementation (see Figure 4.5).[6] These steps contain a number of activities that the team will pursue; they are listed in Table 4.1. Although a detailed description of each of these activities is beyond the scope of this book, let us consider a brief overview.

## Process Direction

As the process design teams begin their work, it becomes clear immediately that they are highly dependent on the directions given by the reengineering leadership group. Each team will be assigned to work on a selected core process, but the members must set the stage for the work to be done. In the process direction step of the model, the team does just that.

Based on the higher-level goals and objectives the team has received, they first develop a vision for the core process that guides them toward the changes needed to achieve this future state. The next task is to decompose the core process into its business processes—including some that may not currently exist. Closely associated with this effort is establishing explicit performance goals for the core process—these will be used to determine whether the redesign options will meet the targets set by senior management.

A critical task for the team is to determine, based on the scope of their effort, who will be affected by the changes they propose and who they should contact and involve in their work. This "stakeholder analysis" will guide the development of a communication plan to keep these parties informed of the work being performed.

The team will develop a project plan that delineates time estimates and resource requirements to support their work. The plan will become part of a presentation to the reengineering

**Figure 4.5**  Process Reengineering—The Heart of Business Reengineering

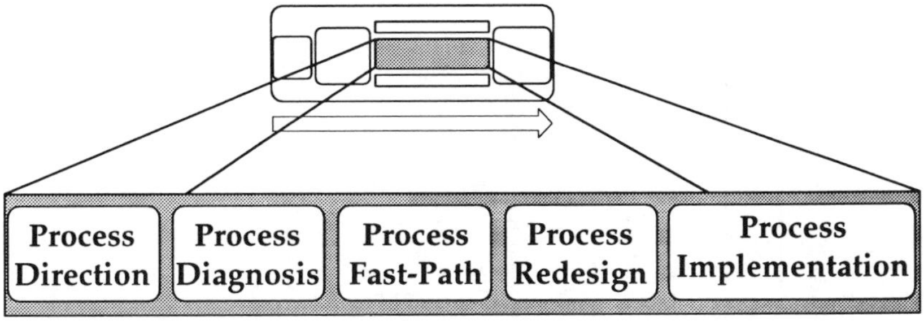

| Process Direction | Process Diagnosis | Process Fast-Path | Process Redesign | Process Implementation |

**Table 4.1** A Process Reengineering Checklist

| Process Direction | Process Diagnosis | Process Fast-Path | Process Redesign | Process Implementation |
|---|---|---|---|---|
| • Create process vision | • Assess current process | • Formulate fast-path strategy | • Create a future process map | • Provide organizational support for implementation |
| • Identify business process and enablers | • Determine change readiness | • Determine fast-path responsibilities | • Develop work flows, metrics, and continuous improvement design | • Implement process enablers |
| • Identify process goals | • Verify customer needs | • Determine current process benefits | • Design process enablers | • Implement process design |
| • Identify stakeholders and develop communications plan | • Benchmark business process | • Develop fast-path plan | • Prototype process and enablers | • Optimize results through continuous improvement process |
| • Prepare project plan | • Perform gap analysis | • Implement plan | • Complete final cost/benefit analysis | |
| • Validate process direction | • Identify process solutions and fast-path opportunities | | • Document final design and transition plan | |
| | • Conduct initial cost/benefit analysis | | • Communicate and secure approval for final design and transition plan | |
| | • Document initial design and transition plan | | | |
| | • Communicate and gain support for initial design and transition plan | | | |

leadership group to gain approval for the team's next steps. Typically, this step lasts between four and six weeks.

## Process Diagnosis

One of the most misunderstood steps in process reengineering comes next. Some people believe it is unnecessary for the team to examine the current environment. However, most teams have not worked together before, and this activity helps them become more efficient and ensures that they all have a common understanding of the current situation. A mixture of internal and external data gathering helps the team decide just how far they need to go to meet their objectives.

The team begins by examining the working environment to understand the operational state of the core process, current measures, and the organizational structure. The team will need to maintain a balanced perspective so that it does not fall into the trap of overanalyzing the present state. Reengineering efforts have failed when teams have pursued detail to the degree that, as Voltaire said, "the perfect becomes enemy to the good." Part of this analysis focuses on the organizational areas surrounding the core process to determine the state of readiness for change. The key dimensions the team will examine have been discussed earlier: leadership, workforce, structure, and process.

*Reengineering efforts have failed when teams have pursued detail to the degree that, as Voltaire said, "the perfect becomes enemy to the good."*

A critical activity in this step involves contact with customers to determine how their needs are being met and to get their reactions to the types of changes the team is considering. Closely related to this work is process benchmarking outside the organization. The team deliberately seeks examples of superior process performance—including examples outside their industry—to see how this performance is achieved from a process and infrastructure perspective. Yogi Berra was right: "You can observe a lot just by watching."

With this knowledge in hand, the team will perform a gap analysis to see just how much change would be required to close it. Based on this assessment, they will explore various process change options to determine which will help them meet their objectives. At this time the team will also identify the "fast-path" options that could be implemented to gain an immediate increase in performance. We will explore the criteria for these options later.

Some initial estimates of costs and benefits, process design, and transition planning will be made in preparation for communicating with stakeholders and to seek further approval from the reengineering leadership group. This step will take eight to twelve weeks.

## Process Fast-Path

Many people who become involved in a reengineering effort underestimate the power of the status quo. Or, as one person put it, "Never turn your back on a bureaucracy." The point is that reengineering has no constituency except at the top of the organization—and these people are very concerned about whether they have made the right choice. The "fast-path" step is next because CEOs have little tolerance for long, drawn out efforts with nothing to show until the very end.[7] They would like assurance that this investment is going to yield a benefit—and some measurable progress to hold up to the inevitable critics who will dog them about why such turbulence is necessary. The fast-path step allows the team to identify and pursue improvement that is achievable in the near term without impeding its reengineering assignment.

Most organizations—certainly those in the health care industry—cannot wait years for improvement. In reality, a large number of problems are well-known throughout the organization, but they may have lacked a sponsor or justification to deal with them. Reengineering offers both. The teams are in a good position to identify and evaluate issues that can be dealt with in a relatively short period of time, with minimal commitment of resources, and without disrupting the work the team has before it.

The team's activities in this step include determining which fast-path issues make sense to pursue from a strategic perspective, offering a cost-benefit analysis of the potential outcomes, estimating the resource requirements, and setting in motion the implementation activity. Often the implementation effort is handled by others outside the team, but the team monitors the effort closely because such changes can and often do influence the broader core process design outcomes. The criteria applied to choosing fast-path options include the following:

- **Source of immediate visible gain**: Why pursue an option that may take as long or longer than the reengineering effort to see a payoff? The payoff should occur in no more than a few months—preferably in a few weeks.

- **Minimal resource requirement**: This is a touchy issue because reengineering demands the "cream of the crop" as team participants. There will be some debate over what further resource commitment the organization would be willing to make to pursue its options. People outside the team could be asked to take this on.

- **Potential redesign support**: The options chosen must not become future obstacles to the redesign effort. On the contrary; the teams will find obstacles that, unless addressed in the short term, could actually impede the redesign effort. At a minimum, pursuing them will give the team some organizational endorsement for creating a more effective and positive work climate.

- **Won't disrupt reengineering effort**: The bottom line for all of this effort is that it should not keep the team from doing what they are supposed to be doing—reengineering a core process. If the organization begins to focus on short-term fixes, the team may never complete its work.

## Process Redesign

In the fourth step, the team develops the details behind the redesign of the core process. This detailed work ensures the organization can actually make such a change and realize the benefit from it.

The team begins by mapping the future core process and underlying business processes. This done, they pursue a detailed examination of the future work flow within the business processes. This will set the stage for decisions regarding infrastructure and measurements.[8] The measures are often described as the "voice" of the process. They are leading indicators of performance at stages before customers receive the outcome. It will also be necessary to identify specific performance measurements for the core process.

The team will need to determine the extent to which the four key infrastructure dimensions need to be realigned to support the redesigned process. In addition, the team sets in motion information technology activity to support the process change. This will likely include system applications, changes in architecture, and helping to create prototypes to test the core process design.[9] Prototypes can offer significant value to a reengineering effort by creating a protected environment for testing out design options. They come in several varieties, as shown in Figure 4.6, and may range on a continuum of "realness" from conceptual discussion to actual real-world piloting of the redesigned process. The following are common uses of prototypes:

- **Concept**: The conceptual option is generally used after the preliminary design of the process is in hand. This allows for a test of technology and serves to educate others, and explore other possibilities in a low-risk manner.
- **Early design**: The early design begins to show an actual working environment, where elements of technology and work design are put together to see how they would work.

**Figure 4.6** The Prototype Continuum

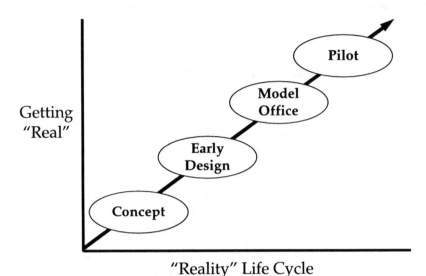

Getting
"Real"

Concept

Early
Design

Model
Office

Pilot

"Reality" Life Cycle

- **Model office:** The model office stage is a sheltered working environment where everything is done to replicate the actual conditions—except exposure to actual interactions with customers. It creates a realistic preview of new circumstances. It is possible to simulate a great deal of potential interaction under these conditions—including the involvement of customers and other stakeholders.
- **Pilot:** The pilot is a "real" working environment used to validate that the new process design and technical systems meet business objectives. Although success at this stage helps guarantee acceptance, the pilot must be seen as occurring in a real and significant part of the business or it will be subject to criticism for being too far removed from the heart of the business.

The final cost-benefit analysis, transition planning, and stakeholder communication occurs before the team goes before the reengineering leadership group for a final approval to implement the change. This fourth step can take eight to twelve weeks.

### Process Implementation

In the fifth and final step of process reengineering, the team prepares the organization for the process design change. Remember, though, that the implementation of this change is subject to the coordination efforts of the reengineering leadership group. The leadership group must see to it that the process design changes occur in a manner that is in the best interest of the business.

Assuming the reengineering leadership group has given its approval, the team provides organizational support for the change through education, redeployment of people to new positions, and so on. This sets the stage for the actual implementation. Some opt for the "big bang" approach and others phase in change slowly. The determining factor is the critical need of the business at that point in time. The process enablers, information technology and various organizational change initiatives (e.g., policy change, management development, resistance management), are put into play.

*Some opt for the "big bang" approach and others phase in change slowly.*

Finally, the team puts into place the continuous improvement infrastructure to ensure that the change they have designed is monitored and changed over time to meet the organization's performance objectives. This is where reengineering and quality management (e.g., TQM/CQI) come together to benefit the organization. This final step can take six months or longer, depending on the scope of the team's effort.

## Process Redesign Tools

The enormity of the work of process teams can be made much easier through training and the use of tools. Some of these tools are shown in Table 4.2.

Over the years, the early quality circle tools (e.g., histograms and Pareto charts) evolved into quality worklife tools and then into TQM/CQI tools. Some people think that their next manifestation is as reengineering tools. TQM/CQI tools are clearly needed in the process implementation step of reengineering, but they do not

| | |
|---|---|
| • Process visioning | • Fast-path analysis |
| • Stakeholder analysis | • Process mapping |
| • Project planning | • Process solutions |
| • Flowcharting | • Communication plan |
| • Change readiness | • Gap analysis |
| • Customer requirements | • Transition plan |
| • Benchmarking | • Prototypes |
| • Infrastructure requirements | • TQM/CQI |
| • Infrastructure solutions | • Cost-benefit analysis |

**Table 4.2**
Process Reengineering Tools

often overlap with reengineering tools. In fact, the earlier tools simply did not sufficiently address business processes. This was certainly true in the areas of benchmarking, customer require-ments, infrastructure requirements, change readiness, and several others. Although a detailed discussion of specific tools is beyond our scope here, we want to emphasize that process redesign teams need access to instruments that are intended for reengineering not just something relabeled out of convenience. Just as reengineering is distinct from other approaches, so too are the tools to support.

## INTEGRATE TECHNICAL SOLUTIONS

Returning to our business reengineering model we come to the information technology component.[10] As noted in Chapter 3, information technology has too often been used to automate inefficient business processes or has been brought in too late in the pursuit of performance improvement. In reengineering, organizations must use the power of technology differently.

### Deduction/Induction

Anyone who has been through a Kepner-Tregoe problem-solving course comes away with the indelible memory of deductive prob-lem solving. Such thinking is common within organizations. For example, one organization insisted that all executive discussions use a "Nine-Step Approach" to guide problem-solving exchanges. Unfortunately, what is needed is a shift toward inductive logic—that is, identifying a solution and then seeking out the problems it can solve. Most problems aren't even recognized because we accept them as "the way things are" instead of as opportunities for change. Few would have even conceived of frozen orange juice in 1914. Carbon paper solved the need to make multiple copies while typing. Why didn't anyone ask how to make copies after typing? Because it was considered impossible. In both cases, technology—refrigeration and photocopiers—offered an opportunity few would have imagined. This is the essence of how reengineering views technology. These new possibilities can turn business economics on its head—supply creates demand.

### Doing What Can't Be Done

Information technology is applied so often to what already exists that few consider its power to allow us to do things differently. Who ever thought to ask a package to tell where it is? Why not expect a car to tell when it has been in an accident? Couldn't the use of information be separated from having to be in fixed locations? The point is that reengineering needs to bring such possibilities to the table at the same time process redesigns are being considered. However, this approach is the reverse of what we normally observe within a business environment dominated by deductive logic.

## Rule Breaking

The term "paradigm shift" refers to a sharp break with historic assumptions about how things ought to be. In this same spirit, reengineering uses information technology to seek out competitive advantage that requires breaking rules that have governed business operations.

Consider the impact of information technology that makes global capitation possible. As complex as it is, this approach to accounting is now within the grasp of health care organizations, and it will cause a break with longstanding rules. For example, the old rule that health care is a response to illness becomes health care is a way to keep people well. The rule that physician income is derived primarily from acute care becomes physician income is derived from establishing alternate advice systems that deal with routine, same day illness. The use of technology allowing optimal use of outcomes data will shift the control of utilization of resources and cost away from utilization review committees and toward giving all patients high-quality care. Technology that allows data to be in more than one place at a time challenges rules supporting centralized paper-based repositories of information. Increased use of artificial intelligence technology breaks the rule that only experts can do complex work.

## Marriage of Convenience

Organizations spend more money on information technology than they do on other forms of change. Because high major expenditures often require senior-level approval, these commitments are rarely changed once a decision has been made. In contrast, we have seen many other less capital-intensive approaches jettisoned at the first sign of organizational discomfort. The implication for reengineering is that the survival of the effort may hinge on its relationship to the commitment of funds for information technology application.[11] Although this is a cynical view of how to bring about organizational change, the political logic is inescapable.

## Health Care Technology

Some people argue that any significant change in the delivery of health care is based on how information is acquired, managed, and used. There are numerous areas where this technology is already gaining significant attention in health care, including

- Wireless data networks
- Integrated administrative systems
- Electronic data interchange
- Severity measurement
- Electronic patient records
- SmartCards
- Portable case management
- Remote access patient information.

The use of information lies at the heart of the challenges being faced by health care businesses. Those who face the need for radical cost management will need to document real cost savings and evaluate patient management. The innovative use of technology is essential. Market differentiation based on quality will require that businesses capture outcome measures and provide them to their customers, including payers, employee benefits managers, and trust fund administrators.[12]

## COORDINATE IMPLEMENTATION WITH CONTINUOUS IMPROVEMENT

Some people suggest that the only sensible pace in revolution is "all at once." These same people argue that one need not pay attention to an organization's history or understand current processes. Others argue that organizations can only change through evolution.[13] This is one of the useless debates that can distract organizations from pursuing a reengineering effort.

In reality, organizations—particularly large ones—need a certain amount of time to institute change. They need a reengineering leadership group to acknowledge the disruptive potential of reengineering and how important it is to develop an overarching plan to help the organization make the transition to a new environment. The plan should include information and recommendations regarding how best to lead the organization to the new environment. While this is a sensible thing to do if there is only one process team, it becomes *critical* when more than one team exists. The plan must give careful attention to coordinating the implementation and determining the trade-offs of making certain changes within selected periods of time.

Preparing an organization for change actually begins with early communication and demonstrated changed behavior by those in leadership positions. This leadership must continue throughout the reengineering effort, and it intensifies significantly at the time of implementation when the organization must ensure that training, education, and resources are available. It also takes strong leaders to accept and respond to the probability that people will leave their previous positions or the organization.

One cannot sustain a revolution indefinitely. Monitoring the implementation of the redesigned core processes and subsequent organization performance can be facilitated with the tools and methods associated with quality management (e.g., statistical process control).[14] Gathering information will make it possible for the organization to sustain continuous process improvement until it is time to reengineer again.

## CHANGE MANAGEMENT

Anyone who thinks that reengineering is a mechanistic lock step, an antiseptic approach that results in an orderly and rational path to change, will find life unkind. In fact, the hardest part of reengineering has nothing to do with creative process redesign or applying the enabling power of information technology. Rather, it is the effort to get a large number of people to accept the need for change and modify their behavior to meet its demands.

Being able to identify the magnitude of change needed in the organization and to assess the organization's readiness to undertake it are two key activities that should occur before an organization ever commits itself to any change effort—particularly reengineering. The organization's reaction to change will reflect current management practices and the legitimate concerns of people who sense that what has been familiar, predictable, and within their sphere of influence is likely to disappear. People in positions of authority must come to accept their role in leading a change process. This means adding a new responsibility to their business repertoire—one that cannot be delegated.

Recent management literature has pointed out the features and advantages of establishing a "learning organization."[15] In the context of reengineering, building a learning organization means building in expectations and support systems that encourage access to external knowledge, and using this knowledge to adapt to change and create a competitive advantage. A "learning" workforce *is* the new competitive advantage. From a reengineering perspective, this shift in perspective is essential for supporting the radical process redesign that leads to a new working environment. We will return to a more detailed discussion of change management issues in Chapter 7, including the identification and use of "change levers" to support a reengineering effort.

*A "learning" workforce is the new competitive advantage.*

## SUMMARY

The application of reengineering to a health care organization can benefit from lessons learned in other contexts. One of these lessons is that successful reengineering includes, but must look beyond, process redesign. New processes ultimately lead to the creation of a new organization, but getting there requires the organizationwide perspective that we call *business reengineering.*

Business reengineering calls for top management to create the direction for the organization, to support the work performed by design teams, and to oversee the progress and implementation of the reengineering effort. Key components of the effort include developing the process structure, establishing a governing body, selecting teams, and orchestrating support for these teams. Particular attention must be paid to the roles and responsibilities of those within the reengineering governing structure, including the reengineering leadership group, the process owner(s), the reengineering czar, process teams, and a pool of resources to support the teams.

As part of the business reengineering process, the organization's infrastructure and the integration of technical solutions are evaluated and applied to issues such as the redirection of recruitment and selection criteria and performance measurement. Technical solutions need to be accompanied by a shift in thinking that puts emphasis on inductive logic—that is, offering solutions that can support options yet to be considered.

*Process reengineering* follows a five-step model to establishing teams. The steps are (1) setting the direction for the team, (2) diagnosing the current situation, (3) identifying "quick hit" opportunities, (4) redesigning a core process to achieve a quantum leap in performance, and (5) implementing the change.

Chapter 5 will take a closer look at processes within a health care organizational environment. We will examine several general design options that have been found to be successful in producing significant gains in performance.

### Notes

1. There has been a growing realization that reengineering tends to falter without addressing organizational issues. For more detail on this point see R. Fischer, R. Canion 1992–1993, "Beyond Re-Engineering, Beyond Outsourcing: Business Integration—The Next Natural Step," *Professional Review* (Winter): 18–20; T. H. Davenport, 1993, *Process Innovation* (Boston: Harvard Business School Press); M. Hammer and J. Champy, 1993, *Reengineering the Corporation* (New York: Harper Business).

2. We will provide additional discussion of resistance and how to overcome it. One particularly interesting treatment of this topic can be found in S. Stanton, M. Hammer, and B. Power, 1992, "From Resistance to Results: Mastering the Organizational Issues of Reengineering," *Insights Quarterly* (Fall): 6–15.

3. For additional discussion of this type of structure, see the Hammer and Champy book and the T. H. Davenport book cited in note 1.

4. One of the more sensitive issues in reengineering is the amount of time that senior executives should commit. For a particularly useful discussion, see G. Hall, J. Rosenthal, and J. Wade, 1993, "How to Make Reengineering *Really* Work," *Harvard Business Review* 71 (November–December): 119–31.

5. The use of internal expertise to address infrastructure change depends on how the organization views its capability in this area. For a discussion of this issue, see D. Ulrich and D. Lake, 1990, *Organizational Capability* (New York: John Wiley & Sons). Patient account management can play a key role within a reengineering effort. See G. D. Kissler, 1995, "Reengineering Patient Account Management," *The Journal of Patient Account Management* (January): 12–15.

6. A casual review of the reengineering literature will find several approaches offered to guide the work of process teams. See T. Furey, 1993, "A Six-Step Guide to Process Reengineering," *Planning Review* 21 (March–April): 20–23; B. D. Harrison, 1993, "A Methodology for Reengineering Businesses," *Planning Review* 21 (March–April): 6–11; H. J. Johansson, P. McHugh, A. J. Pendlebury, and W. Wheeler III, 1993, *Business Process Reengineering* (New York: John Wiley); and J. N. Lowenthal, 1994, *Reengineering the Organization: A Step-by-Step Approach to Corporate Revitalization* (Milwaukee, WI: ASQC Quality Press).

7. We were not surprised to find that someone was tempted to claim that reengineering could be done even more rapidly than what generally occurs. See, for example, J. I. Rosen and S. A. Stanton, 1993, "The Rapid Approach to Reengineering," *Insights Quarterly* (Fall): 26–39. Unfortunately, what is described is not reengineering. It is, instead, taking advantage of opportunities that will arise during the reengineering effort. Some people view the phased-in benefits of reengineering as being "rapid," but we think this is largely an illusion created for political purposes. Large-scale organization change—however packaged for public consumption—takes time.

8. The importance of measurement in reengineering has been mentioned in Chapter 2. For additional discussion of this issue, see C. Meyer, 1994, "How the Right Measures Help Teams Excel," *Harvard Business Review* 72 (May–June): 95–103; and R. H. Schaffer and H. A. Thomson, 1992, "Successful Change Programs Begin with Results," *Harvard Business Review* 70 (January–February): 80–89.

9. For additional discussion on the use of prototypes, see P. Jordan, 1993, "Testing Simulations Offer a Low-Cost, No-Risk Preview," *Enterprise* (July): 36–40.

10. Throughout our discussions, we have emphasized the role of information technology in reengineering. The following sources

offer additional support for this view: R. I. Benjamin and E. Levinson, 1993, "A Framework for Managing IT-Enabled Change," *Sloan Management Review* (Summer): 23–33; T. H. Davenport and J. E. Short, 1990, "The New Industrial Engineering Information Technology and Business Process Redesign," *Sloan Management Review* (Summer): 11–26; R. D. Helppie, 1992, "A Time for Reengineering," *Computers in Healthcare* 13 (January): 22–24; D. Mankin, T. Bikson, B. Gutek, and C. Stasz, 1988, "Managing Technological Change: The Process Is Key," *Datamation*, 15 September, 69–80; D. Morris and J. Brandon, 1992, "Reengineering: More than Meets the Eye," *Computers in Healthcare* 13 (November): 52–54; A. Rai and D. Paper, 1994, "Successful Reengineering through IT Investment," *Information Strategy* (Summer): 18–23; and R. Woolfe, 1992, "The Path to Strategic Alignment," *Indications* 9 (2): 1–13.

11. One of the political realities associated with reengineering is that it often requires a "hook" to keep it from disappearing at the first sign of resistance. For additional discussion on this issue, see G. Harrar, 1994, "Talking Reality," *Enterprise* (January): 20–23.

12. See R. H. Eskow, 1993, "Collection, Correction, Application: The Information Cycle in Managed Healthcare," in P. Boland, ed., *Making Managed Healthcare Work* (Gaithersburg, MD: Aspen Publishers): 445–78. Eskow offers the following point: "Healthcare organizations will need to organize all their information into one centralized system, a health information network, that can make full use of the information being captured. Hospitals, physician offices, utilization review departments, claims processing offices, and financial analysts all capture and use information which represents aspects of the covered population's health."

13. For an example of this point of view, see P. A. Strassman, 1994, "The Hocus-Pocus of Reengineering," *Across the Board* 31: 35–38.

14. The relationship between quality programs and reengineering is discussed further in the following sources: G. K. Gulden and R. H. Reck, 1992, "Combining Quality and Reengineering Efforts for Process Excellence," *Information Strategy: The Executive's Journal* 8 (Spring): 10–16; S. Overman, 1994, "Reengineering, TQM Team for Results," *Society for Human Resource Management/HR News*, (May): 1–4; W. Wachel, 1994, "Reengineering: Beyond Incremental Change," *Healthcare Executive* 9 (July–August): 18–21.

15. For additional information on the concept of the "learning organization," see D. A. Garvin, 1993, "Building a Learning Organization," *Harvard Business Review* 71 (July–August): 78–91; T. Greenwood, A. Wasson, and R. Giles, 1993, "The Learning Organization: Concepts, Processes, and Questions," *Performance & Instruction* (April): 7–11; and P. M. Senge, 1990, *The Fifth Discipline* (New York: Doubleday).

# In Search of Processes

*We will burn that bridge when we come to it.*

A redesign team member

**A**N ORGANIZATION'S struggle to identify its core processes can be a truly pathetic sight—kind of like watching people in a shopping mall staring at those pictures that contain a "hidden" three-dimensional image. For reengineering teams, an equally daunting challenge is to come up with creative redesign options. To help with both, this chapter presents a number of core processes and supporting business processes within the health care industry as well as several redesign approaches with applications in health care.

## KEY CAPABILITIES—REVISITED

The concept of key capabilities was defined in Chapter 2 as the strategic alignment and focus of an organization's core processes to create a competitive advantage by delivering measurable value to a customer. Pursuing health care reengineering will require understanding how to identify these capabilities and their relationship to processes.

### Principles of Key Capabilities

To begin, let us consider some of the principles behind key capabilities:

- Processes are the "building blocks."
- They must lead to superior value to the customer.

- They demand investment in the organizational infrastructure.
- The CEO is the champion of key capabilities.[1]

Now consider how these principles support our definition. First, one constructs a key capability out of processes (the core processes and their underlying business processes within a health care organization). Second, the grouping of processes can only be called a key capability if it leads to a judgment by a customer that superior value has been delivered. Internal efficiency considerations are not sufficient criteria for claiming a key capability.

Next we see a principle that is often overlooked—the investment in organizational infrastructure to support the process activity that underpins a key capability. The infrastructure includes information technology, human resources systems, and other support activity. Finally, because key capabilities cross functional lines, they become the responsibility of the most senior level of management in the organization. An effort to delegate this responsibility would lead to reengineering failure.

The value of key capabilities comes from what they allow an organization to do. In short, a key capability translates into the organization's ability to do the following:

- Develop a cost structure to enable competitive pricing
- Offer consistent product or service quality
- Gain insight into customer needs
- Exploit emerging markets
- Enter new businesses
- Incorporate new ideas into innovation
- Provide customers access to high-quality service
- Create an environment where lessons are learned from the market and from within the organization.

It is easy to understand how success in health care is tied to success in these areas. Moreover, this accomplishment is not a chance occurrence. An organization does not accidentally distinguish itself. Rather, it actively seeks opportunities and uses its relationships with its external environment to learn. The interplay among key areas of the organization is orchestrated in a fashion that allows innovation and takes advantage of business opportunities.

## Organizations Demonstrating Key Capabilities

We have seen several businesses demonstrate key capabilities that give them strategic advantage over their competitors.[2] Some of these are listed below:

| Organization | Key Capability |
|---|---|
| Kaiser-Permanente | Integrated service delivery |
| Medical Equipment Company | On-site service reps |
| Wal-Mart | Cross-docking |
| Honda | Dealer management |
| Banc One | Personalized service |
| Lee Memorial Hospital | Patient-focused care |

Few names are as recognizable as Kaiser-Permanente in the area of integrated service delivery. By combining the benefits of insurance with care delivery skills and superior facilities, this organization set a standard for providing cost-effective health care that has only recently been challenged.[3]

Medical Equipment Company found that the renewal of its customer contacts had less to do with order size than it did with on-site representation. These representatives came to know the customer and its challenges well enough to anticipate supply needs and were in a position to act in the timely manner that customers needed and valued.

Most of us can remember when there was a Sears and a K-Mart but no Wal-Mart. Now Wal-Mart has taken a lead position in its market, and one of its key capabilities is inventory management. "Cross-docking" is a devilishly difficult set of processes that allows Wal-Mart to receive goods at its warehouses and, within 48 hours, move them to individual stores without incurring storage costs. This capability gives the chain a distinct price advantage over its competitors.

Honda's relationship to its dealers is similar to that between McDonald's and its suppliers. Honda takes an active role in educating dealers in basic business principles and the management of the enterprise. This has led to a stronger dealer network, in terms of meeting customer needs while maintaining financial stability, than is generally found among Honda's competitors.

Banc One has moved decidedly in favor of offering banking services to individual customers in a manner once reserved only for "high roller" types. These services include providing investment information and offering access to investment options. The company has combined training for front-line people with substantial investment in information technology.

Lee Memorial Hospital in Fort Meyers, Florida, is one of several hospitals that have embraced the patient-focused approach to health care delivery. This approach is based on the assumption that care should be brought to patients—not vice versa. The next section illustrates some of the features of patient-focused care that make it a key capability in health care.

## Patient-Focused Care as a Key Capability

Let us begin by examining some of the key principles behind patient-focused care.[4]

- **Reaggregation:** Patients should be grouped in centers or units based on their need for similar health care resources, such as equipment, physician specialists, housing, and other requirements.

- **Redeployment:** When justified by a patient center's utilization, health care resources (such as equipment, supplies, specialized clinical, administrative, and support labor, and clinical and administrative processes) should be decentralized and brought closer to the patient.

- **Simplification:** Processes affecting the patient center should be simplified to reduce or eliminate steps that do not contribute to the desired outcome.

- **Flexible, cross-trained jobs:** Jobs in patient centers should be redefined to include many different functions that workers are cross-trained to perform.

- **Self-directed teams:** The organizational structure of each patient center should include self-directed teams with well-defined goals and the responsibility, authority, and skills to achieve those goals.

- **Organizational architecture:** The organizational architecture (including the organization's structure, culture, style, and communication mechanisms) outside the center should be redesigned to support the center.

Figure 5.1 shows the structure of patient care centers chosen by Lee Memorial Hospital. To achieve a necessary critical mass of skills within each area, it was necessary to cross-train phlebotomists, transporters, respiratory therapists, radiology technicians, physical therapists, occupational therapists, dietary staff, admitting staff, and nurses and nurse aides.

An early analysis found that each of these clinical professionals had a large caseload but was responsible for only a fraction of the care received by a patient. The new structure brings them together within each cluster so that a whole matrix of care is within the line of sight of each team member. Needless to say, all this cross-training often runs counter to the culture of a hospital. Professional licensing and identification with one's own department, for example, often lead to turf disputes. To create, integrate, and orchestrate the delivery of care, many hospitals hire a case manager who focuses on individual patient cases.

**Figure 5.1** Structure of Patient-Focused Care

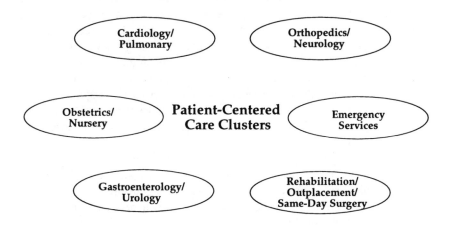

Hospitals pursuing this key capability report results that are quite impressive.[5] For example, Multicare Health System in Washington State is making a transition from traditional delivery to what it calls a patient-focused work design. It has simplified work and documentation, and improved clinical efficiency by redefining multiskilled roles—resulting in a savings of $6 million in 1992–1993. Lee Memorial has found less reported stress among its hospital staff and an increase in satisfaction among doctors. Their patient satisfaction surveys indicate a 13 to 17 percent increase in customers' satisfaction with the quality of care. The length's of hospital stays (along with noise levels!) have been reduced. There has been a decrease in turnaround time for tests. Other patient-focused hospitals report productivity gains in the form of decreased paperwork, improved scheduling, reductions in process steps, and less time spent on noncore care delivery (e.g., chasing information).

Patient-focused care is not without its critics. They argue that cross-training has its limits, it doesn't lower costs, and that the capital investment can be considerable. Indeed, as a key capability, patient-focused care faces many of the challenges that we have discussed within the broader context of health care reengineering. In concept it is sound, but the implementation leaves much to be desired. In Chapter 6 we will discuss the organizational commitment needed for success.

## HEALTH CARE PROCESSES

Health care organizations need to identify the processes that will be the primary focus of their reengineering. Recall that a *core process* is a group of interrelated, measurable, cross-functional, business processes that creates an output valued by the customer. A *business process* is a group of measurable linked activities that transforms an input into an output valued by the customer. Core processes operate at a higher strategic level and create output valued by a customer because of the way the business processes are orchestrated. The business processes themselves operate at the next level and are often viewed as being functionally anchored—a judgment that has been challenged by reengineering's insistence on looking at an organization in terms of its horizontal activity.

Figure 5.2 is a graphic representation of the relationship between core processes and business processes. This relationship has two important features. First, core processes are aggregates of interrelated business processes. We will provide some specific examples of these later.

The second feature is less easily understood. A business process can—and often does—support more than one core process. This might not *seem* like a particularly difficult concept, but it is surprising how often it goes unnoticed until separate reengineering teams begin their work. Potential conflicts between these efforts must be resolved by senior management.

The reengineering leadership group must ensure that the work done by process design teams is coordinated. One of the areas that must be monitored closely is changes to business processes that could impede the work done by other process teams. In short, it is unlikely that the same "fix" will be chosen for the same business process by two different teams. However, when business

**Figure 5.2**    Relationship between Care Process and Business Process

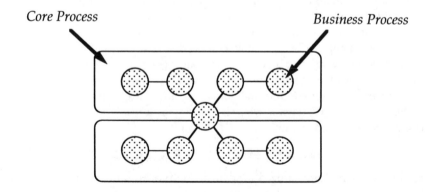

*Core Process*                                     *Business Process*

processes *are* shared by more than one team, the teams will need trade-off decisions by senior management and judgments from the reengineering leadership group.

Let us now turn to some specific examples of core processes and the business processes that support them.[6] Some of these can also be found in other industries, but we will emphasize those with particular relevance to the health care industry.

**Core Process:** Preventive medical care

**Business Processes:**

- Capture medical information
- Integrate information into patient records
- Compare current status with guidelines
- Notify doctors/patients
- Service delivery
- Update patient record
- Notify patient of results.

One of the major shifts in health care, driven largely by capitation, is increased emphasis on keeping people well versus returning them to health. Our first core process reflects this new perspective. It was developed by an HMO reengineering team. The core process, preventive medical care, is given a label that describes the beginning and ending business processes. The business processes begin with capturing medical information and conclude with notifying the patient of the results of the preventive care. This core process will almost certainly become more commonly recognized and pursued for competitive advantage—after the immediate cost wars have subsided.

Another key business process is education that leads to a willingness to alter one's lifestyle. Less than 4 percent of the decline in mortality between 1900 and 1973 resulted from medical measures. The real contributors to declining mortality in the early twentieth century were better housing, hygiene, and nutrition. You would think that a capitated environment, in which a higher volume of patients means *lower* profits, would change the mindset of so many who cling tenaciously to a disappearing model of care delivery. Daniel J. Isenberg said, "In general, the human mind is conservative. Long after an assumption is outmoded, people tend to apply it to novel situations." *Success* is measured by how many patients receive health care, not how many are kept healthy.

*The real contributors to declining mortality in the early twentieth century were better housing, hygiene, and nutrition.*

**Core Process:** Service realization

**Business Processes:**

- Research and target marketing
- Collaborative development/design
- Advertising and promotion
- Service setup and testing
- Service evaluation.

Many of us are familiar with product development as an important process in business. It has also been identified as a core process in a health care organization pursuing an integrated service delivery capability. They labeled it "service realization" to convey a broader scope than just development. As the supporting business processes suggest, the realization of service begins with early research and reaches past the delivery of the service to an analysis to determine its value to customers.

**Core Process:** Inpatient services

**Business Processes:**

- Preadmission care
- Admission
- Therapeutics
- Service delivery
- Case management.

A reengineering team within a medical center faced the challenge of making high-quality ambulatory care available to its customers. Because inpatient services had been one of their primary revenue sources, the team sought to redesign this core process to reduce resource requirements and streamline to increase profit margin. This process is broad in scope and the supporting business processes cross functional lines, making it an ideal candidate for a reengineering effort.

**Core Process:** Outpatient services

**Business Processes:**

- Diagnostics services
- Scheduling
- Treatment services
- Ambulatory surgery
- Results reporting
- Patient accounting.

Outpatient services was identified as a core process by a reengineering team within a hospital that wanted to become a cost-based competitor. The hospital made the decision to redesign how it delivered outpatient services. Figure 5.3 shows the cycle of events within the hospital's outpatient services. The cycle begins when a patient is seen by a physician and a decision is made regarding the treatment event. The next phase is a series of pre-event activities:

- **Scheduling:** Setting up an appointment for the event
- **Ordering:** Arranging for equipment, tests, and staff for the event
- **Registration:** Obtaining necessary patient information, insurance, and so on
- **Insurance precertification:** Gaining the insurer's agreement to cover the event
- **Financial counseling:** Reviewing patient's obligation.

The critical task the hospital faces is the centralization of these activities, which are now fragmented across several areas. They intend to combine the first three into one activity and set a dollar threshold for seeking precertification. Their goals include creating a more predictable cost structure to allow for a credit card–like transaction instead of the current financial counseling. They also intend to gain cycle time improvement in these areas as well as reduce the time it takes to report results back to a physician.

**Core Process:** Medical services management

**Business Processes:**
- Provider servicing
- Health care decision support
- Disease and quality management
- Practice and case management
- Wellness education and care assistance.

A major health care insurer has identified medical services management as critical to supporting its provider relationship capability. As we can see from its associated business processes, this business is faced with the almost certain fragmentation of business process activities across the current organization. In fact, the success of this particular business in terms of the core process will most likely be decided by how it changes its relationships with its customers. Many of the business processes will force a serious reconsideration of how this business defines the boundaries that

**Figure 5.3**  Outpatient Services Cycle

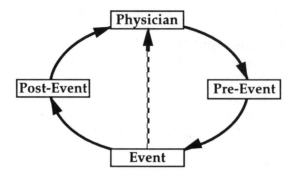

separate it from its market. They will need to determine what core processes would have to be combined to allow the organization to become a "health care integrator."

These examples of health care processes demonstrate how reengineering teams have come to view their organizations. As they seek to identify and redesign these processes, they find this is a particularly challenging task for another reason. The processes within a service industry like health care differ from those in other industries.[7] In particular, health care organizations find it more difficult to determine the owner of the process, to decide where to draw process boundaries, to establish control points, to measure output, and to gain support for corrective actions that go beyond merely reacting to an immediate problem.

## HEALTH CARE REDESIGN STRATEGIES

The identification of health care processes, while challenging, pales in comparison to the choice of redesign options. The good news is that several examples exist as models to help a team guide its efforts. The less than good news is that the team will have to do this with a minimum of assistance. This is because although the redesign strategies are general, their applications are not. The application will have to address the uniqueness of the individual health care organization. Nevertheless, teams can benefit from a review of several redesign strategies that have been considered elsewhere.

### Relocate Work to/from Customers

Examples of how business organizations relocate work to or from customers include ATMs, unfinished furntiure, and do-it-yourself legal documents. This approach to health care includes giving patients the means to handle certain therapies (e.g., home IV therapy) and preparing themselves for provider contact. Some organizations are considering asking their medical suppliers to manage their inventory, another redefinition of organizational boundaries.

## Eliminate Intermediaries

Eliminating intermediaries—or removing the "middle man"— can often be done through the use of information technology. In the insurance industry this means bypassing independent agents and seeking direct customer contact. In health care, the elimination of intermediarie's means providing customers with direct access to information that historically was delivered in person. Test results and other provider feedback can be accessible by phone if the patient is offered a code to ensure protection of private information. Another example is an attempt to remove the admitting area in its current form. One suggestion is that a large number of ambulatory surgery patients could bypass current admissions and have this done at bedside.

## Achieve Benefits of Parallel Activity and Sequencing

It is possible to move from conducting activities in a serial fashion to having them done in parallel. In the manufacturing industry customer orders used to get held up because one part of the organization waited for another to indicate its work was done. No one realized that the second group didn't need the input from the first to make its contribution. Until this "assumed dependency" was investigated, response time to customers was just considered normal and beyond significant improvement. A health care example includes the business processes of having multiple access to patient records, so that various ancillary service groups could input results without waiting for others to do so. Drug manufacturers are also beginning to create parallel paths in the process of bringing a new product to market.

## Create Hybrid Centralized and Decentralized Structures

Process design teams have decided against an either/or solution in continuing debate over the merits of centralization versus decentralization. Instead, they have formulated hybrid options, which use information technology to allow for more local access to central information. Examples include bedside terminals that display integrated patient records, material purchasing done via remote terminals that access data in a central database, and centralizing pharmacy activity focused on filling orders, but decentralizing distribution points. Similar arguments lie at the heart of the patient-focused care concept.

## Achieve Greater Efficiency through Rapid Decisions

It is possible to reduce the inefficiency caused by delayed decisions. Within the electronics industry, for example, service cost is reduced substantially by rapidly diagnosing the problem. Within health care, greater efficiencies are revealed in comparisons between the historic provider care delivery process and one called a "problem-oriented system."[8] The traditional process has a provider taking these steps: history, exam, diagnosis, treatment, and check. The problem-oriented system has four features: database, problem formulation, plan, and follow up. The latter provides a better trail of information and can move the process along faster. A second example in health care is the cost incurred because of the reluctance of providers to release a patient from the hospital. Redesign teams found it was necessary to streamline administrative procedures that were keeping physicians from having time for patient contact. The greater their opportunity for contact, the more willing they were to release the patients.

## Achieve Greater Flexibility through Delayed Decisions

Paradoxically, reengineering teams have occasionally found value in slowing down processes. In the clothing industry, Benneton discovered that delaying the dyeing of fabric allowed them to avoid discounting inventory that was out of fashion due to its color. In health care too there are times when a slower decision can allow delaying resource commitments until they are proven necessary. Examples include pursuing noninvasive options prior to surgery and allowing for more time to screen providers before selecting them as members of provider networks.

*The health care industry has only begun to "think out of the box," and future strategies chosen by reengineering teams will make an even greater break with past practices.*

The health care industry has only begun to "think out of the box," and future strategies chosen by reengineering teams will make an even greater break with past practices. Even so, there are no set answers, and teams will have to match their strategies to the performance demands of their organizations. Table 5.1 provides a starting point, with suggestions to help a team recognize appropriate strategies and the outcomes to expect.

**Table 5.1**   Process Design Strategies

| Design Option | When Is This Strategy Appropriate? | What Is the Outcome? |
|---|---|---|
| Relocate work to or from customers | Extensive overhead costs related to coordination or transaction; the two entities have large differences in the size, importance, access, capability | Reduced cost associated with coordination of work activities and "boundary management" enhanced outcome measures |
| Eliminate intermediaries | Interactions between people are not adding sufficient value to justify the cost; customer is unnecessarily reliant on third-party involvement | Improved customer service through automated interaction; reduced cost by moving responsibility boundaries |
| Achieve benefits of parallel activity and sequencing | Activities that don't rely on preceding ones are still not begun until earlier ones are complete; the order of events is not logical | Improved process control through resequencing and/or combining activities |
| Create hybrid centralized and decentralized structures | Duplication of activities occur in multiple locations; lack of adequate coordination or resource allocation capability | Achieved economies of scale or expertise while maintaining optimal customer response/service |
| Achieve greater efficiency through rapid decisions | Delayed decisions result in missed market opportunities and increased costs related to accelerated resource use | Reduced overhead and process time; more efficient "loading" of resource demand; improved customer service |
| Achieve greater flexibility through delayed decisions | Increased cost due to too-early commitments of resources; sunk costs related to process outcomes no longer valued by customer; poor relationships | Reduced cost by designing process to delivery outcomes in sequence that matches information available; greater flexibility |

## SUMMARY

Two of the most significant challenges in health care reengineering are identifying processes to redesign and choosing appropriate redesign strategies. The choice of processes should reflect the key capabilities that will provide the organization with a competitive advantage. A number of core processes and their supporting business processes within the health care industry have been discussed in this chapter. The chapter also highlighted redesign strategies that have been used by reengineering teams in health care.

### Notes

1. For an expanded discussion of capabilities, see G. Stalk, Jr., P. Evans, and L. E. Shulman, 1992, "Competing on Capabilities: The New Rules of Corporate Strategy," *Harvard Business Review* 70 (March–April): 57–69.

2. We have discussed capabilities in Chapter 2. One of the often-cited sources in this area is G. Hamel and C. K. Prahalad, 1994, "Competing for the Future," *Harvard Business Review* 68 (July–August): 122–28.

3. For a discussion of Kaiser-Permanente's current challenges, see G. Anders, 1994, "In Age of the HMO, Pioneer of the Species Has Hit a Rough Patch," *The Wall Street Journal,* 1 December; and D. Azvedo, 1995, "Can the World's Largest Integrated Health System Learn to Feel Small?" *Medical Economics* (23 January): 82–101.

4. Additional details pertaining to patient-focused care can be found in C. Schartner, 1993, "Principles of Patient-Focused Care," *Healthcare Information Management* 7 (Spring): 11–15; and N. C. Troup, 1992, "World Class Healthcare™ Revolutionizing the Way Hospitals Do Business," *Healthcare Information Management* 6 (Winter): 3–8; and D. Zimmerman and J. J. Skalko, 1994, *Reengineering Health Care* (Franklin, WI: Eagle Press).

5. There have been several published descriptions of the success of hospitals pursuing some form of patient-focused care. Among them are C. Dunbar, 1994, "MultiCare Health System Saves Millions of Dollars through Redesigned Care," *Health Management Technology* 15 (July): 22–29; W. D. Nipper and E. Farmer, 1993, "Patient-Focused Hospital: Implementation Results," *1993 HIMSS Conference Proceedings* (2): 26–33; N. Moore and H. Komras, 1993, *Patient-Focused Healing* (San Francisco: Jossey-Bass); and D. Roberts, R. Kremsdorf, J. Tomabeni, and A. K. Tinker, 1993, "Clinical Decision Support at the Bedside: The New Patient-Centered Hospital," *1993 HIMSS Conference Proceedings* (3): 140–51.

6. This section and the one that follows on redesign options were drawn from our health care reengineering workshop. The examples chosen represent the type of issues being addressed within health care organizations and the options being considered by their reengineering teams. For a discussion of redesign options found in other industries, see T. H. Davenport, 1993, *Process Innovation*

(Boston: Harvard Business School Press) and M. Hammer and J. Champy, 1993, *Reengineering the Corporation* (New York: Harper Business).

7. For a comparison of the characteristics of processes in service versus manufacturing processes, see J. Lowenthal, 1994, *Reengineering the Organization: A Step-by-Step Approach to Corporate Revitalization* (Milwaukee, WI: ASQC Quality Press).

8. For a more detailed discussion of this care delivery approach, see H. M. Tufo and H. E. Davis, 1993, "Quality Control in the Delivery of Healthcare in the State of Vermont," in Peter Boland, ed., *Making Managed Healthcare Work* (Gaithersburg, MD: Aspen Publishers).

## CHAPTER 6

# Price of Admission

*Never turn your back on a bureaucracy.*

Anonymous

**M**OST HEALTH care organizations can be described as chaos covered by a thin veneer of order, which may explain the reluctance of management to introduce any significant change. The literature describing the difficulties encountered by organizations attempting to reengineer suggests that they have been unwilling to pay the price of admission. This chapter examines the level of commitment an organization should be prepared to give and looks at several organizations that failed and why. Finally, it presents suggestions for how to determine the "reengineering readiness" of an organization.

## A WALK ON THE POLITICAL SIDE

The previous chapters described the "rational" side of health care reengineering—the statistics and trends indicating the need for change and the documented improvements that result from reengineering. Understanding the conceptual definitions, principles, models, roles, and methodology also helps one understand how reengineering actually works. To all of this we have added health care context to help in applying the approach to this industry. It would be tempting to stop here, wish everyone well, and hope for the best. Doing so would likely lead to additional reengineering failures by well-intentioned organizations. Why? Because most organizations are unable or unwilling to make the commitment needed to change. Although this position may seem overly pessimistic, it is worth emphasizing that one should not pursue health care reengineering without considering the true price of admission.

The "currency" that constitutes this price of admission goes beyond monetary cost. It includes the political issues that arise during the transformation of organizations, most of which can only be addressed by senior management:

## CONFRONTING IGNORANCE

It is surprising how fiercely some executives resist the notion that reengineering is something new—something that they don't already know. By failing to accept this, they justify not investing in an effort to understand more about it. Sometimes people don't know what they don't know. What's worse, if what they don't know doesn't get them into trouble, what they know that ain't so will.

Reengineering involves some challenging concepts, models, and tools that deserve careful attention. It is important that senior management attain some understanding of these features before commitments are made to pursue reengineering. Failing to do this has resulted in many businesses labeling whatever they do as reengineering. Unfortunately, just coming to appreciate the *need* for additional knowledge is not enough.

## WILLINGNESS TO LEARN

Convincing executives to *pursue* knowledge is the second biggest hurdle many organizations encounter. Successful businesses sometimes inadvertently create environments that "punish" any admission that new knowledge is needed. They compound the problem by asserting that any knowledge that *is* needed should be available internally, thus closing the door to external input. In short, they create the classic example of a closed system.

Top executives may be incredibly resistant to pursuing new knowledge. This resistance comes in many forms, including outright denial that knowledge is needed or getting distracted by the label put on the learning process. People have told me—with a straight face—that executives don't need *training*; they need a *seminar* where they can exchange knowledge. Regardless of the label, it is important to do whatever it takes to ensure there is a willingness to participate.

## LINK REENGINEERING TO STRATEGY

One of the primary reasons that top executives need sufficient information about reengineering is that they bear the responsibility for seeing that it is linked to strategy. Far too many performance improvement efforts operate in a vacuum. Actually, avoiding reengineering failure by developing this linkage is not all that difficult.

Figure 6.1 shows a typical strategic planning sequence that begins with an executive team developing likely scenarios their business will face. Next comes a competitive analysis that helps them compare their organization to others in their competitive arena. This comparison frames up a future view for the business and the degree of change required. It also helps move the team to the selection of capabilities and core processes that will support the magnitude and direction of change they seek.

It is impossible to gain the full potential for improvement unless the top executive team takes direct control of this integration of strategy and reengineering. This integration must go beyond traditional strategic planning objectives (organizational, functional, divisional, unit, and individual goals), which reflects the functional structure and mindset that are targeted by reengineering. Rather, organizational goals must reflect a shift toward thinking horizontally. Process goals should be developed to reflect organizational goals and serve to redefine functional and individual goals.[1]

## MANAGING THE ''GRAY ZONE'' ············

When developing an organizational strategy, top management teams draw on internal and external assistance to examine their competitive position within their industry—thus gaining insight

**Figure 6.1** Linking Reengineering to Business Strategy

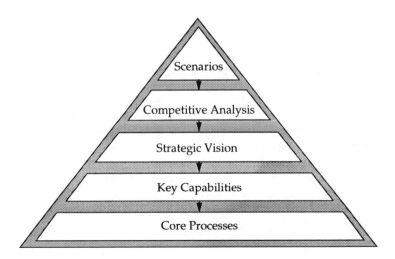

into what it would take to create a sustainable competitive advantage.

The logical next step is to examine what it would take to move the organization in this direction and compare it against current operational capacity. The problem comes in the "gray zone," an area that lies between strategic considerations and required operational performance. At this point, it may be helpful to create a series of scenarios and questions within the context of strategic planning that will serve the needs of teams later asked to reengineer core processes. In short, unless specific understanding of reengineering leads to such discussions within strategic planning, the necessary linkage between the two will not occur.

## EXECUTIVE BEHAVIOR

It is clear that reengineering must be driven from the top of the organization.[2] What may not be clear, however, is what top managers should do to demonstrate their commitment to reengineering. A good place to start is communication.

Many executives appear reluctant to publicly endorse reengineering. Perhaps this is because they fear being asked for clarifications they can't provide. But speaking out forcefully, consistently, and frequently is essential—and it is only the beginning. Top executives have the authority to create incentives for those who take up the challenge of reengineering, and they need to demonstrate their commitment by doing so. In addition, they need to show a willingness to remove those who attempt to impede the effort—or find them a new "home" elsewhere.

It is also important that "executive presence" is demonstrated through appearances at reengineering training sessions, participating in process team review sessions, and otherwise showing forms of behavior that reflect the new values they want reengineering to reinforce.

## PROVIDE ''AIR COVER''

Critical executive behavior includes offering protection to the reengineering effort—particularly at its outset. Reengineering is most vulnerable when resources are requested, when decisions about scope are made, and when priorities are set. Because there is no constituency for this type of change, some will take this opportunity to discredit and stop the reengineering effort. In these circumstances, top management must stand ready to defend the decision to take the organization through reengineering and to make it clear that continued criticism will not be ignored or allowed to distract the effort. Any reengineering effort will have its flaws—the path to success is always under construction—but top management needs to give it time to demonstrate its value. Perhaps the strongest statement a top executive has made regarding a reengineering effort was this: "We will carry our wounded and shoot the stragglers."[3] It doesn't get much clearer than that.

## CREATE A SENSE OF URGENCY

One cannot overemphasize the lethargy that exists within large organizations—particularly those with some past success. Past accomplishments are often viewed as an indication that the organization *used to* know what it was doing! Layer upon layer of procedure evolves, making it nearly impossible to achieve better results. To do so would violate in-bred behaviors. These take the form of long decision approval chains, requiring that no discussions occur without a formal written agenda, insisting that all decisions must be unanimous, and giving greater value to form than substance.

Trying to instill a sense of urgency is critical in a business that has treated the passage of time with indifference. Somehow you have to bring to people's attention the events that are happening outside the organization, the consequences of not taking action, and the opportunities that will be lost as well. This should be coupled with explicit expectations as to what needs to be accomplished, by whom, and within what specified time frame.

## STOP OTHER STUFF

An organization must avoid letting reengineering become just another performance initiative in the competition for finite resources. Unequivocally, reengineering must be the organization's top priority, and as such, it needs to be given the resources required to carry it out. Efforts to pursue change in a different manner, if they compete for resources, must be stopped while reengineering is under way.

Some organizations simply cannot bring themselves to confront the funneling of resources into senior managers' "pet projects." Many are unrelated to the organization's overall business strategy or never demonstrate any tangible benefit. Confronting these projects is a true test of the organization's commitment to reengineering. Others will be watching!

## RECEPTIVE ENVIRONMENT

Over the years we have heard a great deal of discussion about organizational culture and its relationship to success. There are certain characteristics about a working environment that increase the likelihood of reengineering success. For example, reengineering needs an environment where there is a fair amount of trust between employees and management. Past history of successful change increases the chances for another. Has the organization successfully contended with a merger, downsizing, or acquisition? Another key indicator is employee involvement and participation. Team-based involvement toward specific goals and accountability for achieving goals are indications of environments where reengineering is likely to take hold.

## COMMITMENT OF THE BEST AND BRIGHTEST

Staffing of a reengineering effort is usually a sensitive issue. The truth of the matter is that most organizations have a limited amount of what they consider "top talent," and these individuals are guarded jealously. Reengineering needs these top people to fill key roles in the effort. Their participation will be vital to the success of the reengineering leadership group, the governing structure, and the process design teams.

Staffing involves difficult decisions and the way they are made will demonstrate the organization's commitment to reengineering. This is particularly true of the selection of process design team members, because they may spend a long period of time on the team and wind up with totally different positions.

## INTERNAL REENGINEERING EXPERTISE

*The organization needs to accept that no "off-the-shelf" solutions exist and that they must tailor a solution to respond to the unique needs of the business.*

For reengineering to be accepted, it must be "owned" and driven by the organization itself. External consultants can be helpful in terms of their past experience and the tools, methodology, and techniques they can offer. Beyond this, though, the organization needs to accept that no "off-the-shelf" solutions exist and that they must tailor a solution to respond to the unique needs of the business. The use of teams of well-prepared and knowledgeable internal participants (augmented by some "external yeast"), who will maintain control and ownership of the process and outcomes, is the best choice.

## CONFRONT RESISTANCE

"Constructive conflict" is still a rarity within many business organizations. Open displays of disagreement continue to be treated as a sign of poor social breeding or genetic defect. Make no mistake about it, reengineering will bring the critics out of the woodwork, many with legitimate issues that deserve attention. Ignoring dissent is the worse form of change management if you are looking for future buy-in and cooperation. (Recall that a climate fostering open debate was one of Motorola's keys to success.)

On the other hand, a different strategy may be needed to deal with people who have decided to resist the reengineering effort and who actively work to derail it or put up dazzling forms of passive resistance. This behavior should be addressed directly, openly, and swiftly to send a signal that those who choose to pursue it will find life becoming a lot less friendly. We will return to this issue when we discuss the management of change in Chapter 7.

## RISK TAKING

It might be tempting to attribute reengineering failures to chance. Certainly there is an element of risk associated with every action an organization takes, including doing nothing. However, reengineering efforts should not be confused with gambling. Compared to playing a slot machine, it is more like a game of chess—one has considerably more control over the outcome, and applying focused effort can improve the odds of success.

Nevertheless, organizations that are unwilling to take a calculated risk become paralyzed by indecision, thus running an even greater risk. The risk-averse nature of the health care industry makes reengineering success that much harder to achieve. Nearly 50 percent of the Fortune 500 businesses listed in 1980 are no longer in existence; one would have to conclude that Darwin was right. Everyone has the right to choose and survival is only one option.

## STAFFING CHANGE

Recently I worked with an organization that had never laid off a significant number of employees. Further, poor performance often resulted in people being placed in another position rather than being removed. The resulting culture was one in which employment became viewed as an entitlement. When it became clear that reengineering would require a new mix of skills, people became quite uncomfortable. When they realized that the new mix could very well outstrip the capabilities of many of their current employees, they refused to discuss it.

Reengineering seeks, as a primary objective, to help an organization perform more effectively. This often means doing more with fewer people, but it also means you need people who bring more complex skills to more complex jobs. Organizations that pursue reengineering must accept the possibility and prepare the necessary support to manage a transition in its workforce. Retraining should be encouraged where possible, but there are three reasons why it will not always be sufficient. First, some people may not be trainable. Second, the organization may not have the capability of offering the training required. Third, the time frame involved may preclude relying entirely on retraining to meet the skill requirements. In short, you have to be realistic.

## RETHINK ENABLER ROLE OF TECHNOLOGY

Past organizational changes that were driven by information technology (IT) often failed because of the way the technology was introduced, because it tended to focus on current processes without questioning their utility, and because of the organizational disruption that often came as a surprise. Reengineering needs to make use of IT as an enabler. The organization must confront its past use of technology and reconsider its future role, and the people in the IT area will need to be introduced to the role of IT within reengineering so they can support the effort.

Management will need to understand what IT can do to help them "break the rules" and pursue business opportunities that no one ever considered. In addition, they will need to promote a much closer working relationship between IT and line management and a significant shift in mindset about the nature of IT itself.

## MANAGE THE POWER OF CHANGE

There is no doubt that reengineering brings about significant turbulence in an organization. How could anyone expect otherwise, given its cross-functional nature? The issue is not whether or not such turbulence is necessary. Rather, it is that the organization should use this disruption as an opportunity to reposition the organization to take advantage of the change.

This is different from *mastering* change. One might just as well try to master the tide and wind. Rather, it is about seeing the force of change as offering the potential to shift direction and knowing how to gain acceptance and overcome resistance. Chapter 7 will focus on how change management can be woven into the fabric of a reengineering effort.

This discussion of the price of admission should help clarify why many organizations shy away from reengineering. It is not necessarily a bad thing that they do since other approaches to change may offer a better fit to the organization's situation. Those who proceed with reengineering, however, must assess their organization's readiness for such an approach.

## REENGINEERING READINESS

The darker side of reengineering is reflected in the statistics on the percentage of reengineering efforts that fail. The business press reports numbers ranging from 25 to 70 percent.[4] To address this issue, this chapter examines specific cases of failure and what caused them. It also offers a way to assess an organization's readiness for reengineering.

### Beyond Good Intentions

The euphoria associated with the "latest management craze" often manages to dull the reasoning of otherwise capable people. This is certainly understandable when you consider the pressures so many businesses face. For all its promise, reengineering does make considerable demands on organizations, and many try to gain the outcomes from reengineering without taking the steps needed to succeed.

But speaking about reengineering failure in the abstract is not as informative as looking more closely at businesses that have been brave enough to speak out about their shortcomings. This sobering perspective offers a long overdue balance to the hype about reengineering. Some businesses that have found reengineering to be something less than a day at the beach.[5]

- **Citibank N.A.** admits it wasted $50 million in a year-long effort to reengineer its back-office securities processing. Their effort was damaged by trying to simultaneously carry out activities that should have been done sequentially.

- **Xerox's** attempt to reengineer its proposal-order-to-collection process collapsed because it lacked a testbed to prove itself, was burdened by large investment requirements, and lacked support from top stakeholders.

- **American Express** immersed itself in the concept of TQM. The arrival of reengineering sparked a heated debate between two warring factions. The resolution, in essence, was to describe reengineering as a subset of TQM. While American Express battled internally, MasterCard and Visa each forged ahead with a new product.

- **Charles Schwab & Co.** attempted to improve funds delivery through reengineering. It failed to name a process owner, lacked adequate customer focus, was too heavily focused on fixing existing systems, and had an information systems function that was at odds with the reengineering group.

- **St. Francis Regional Medical Center** cited the following reasons for its reengineering failure:
  - Nonconfrontational management style
  - Little cross-functional involvement
  - People chose to retain staff versus pursuing reengineering and risking loss of staff
  - Consultant not given sufficient direction from medical facility
  - Consultant gave insufficient warning about "downside" of effort
  - The "champion" was the CEO, and he left
  - People saw redesign as a way to get more staff
  - Redesign became too narrowly focused (e.g., a "nursing project")
  - Needed a more definitive tool to measure customer satisfaction.

If one accepts the statistics offered in the business literature, the examples of failure cited here are only a fraction of the many reengineering efforts that have been quietly disbanded. Quietly disbanding is common when an organization is faced with embarrassment and disappointment. One can only hope that reengineering was not the best approach to change and that a better one has taken its place. A more likely scenario, however, is that reengineering was the right approach, but the organization was simply not ready to accept its demands. The examples highlighted here only begin to touch upon the causes of reengineering failure.

## Causes of Reengineering Failure

Table 6.1 is a list of the more common causes of reengineering failure.[6]

### Lack of Understanding about Reengineering

Senior executives are too often put in a position of endorsing a reengineering effort without examining it in sufficient detail.

### Inadequate Management of Resistance

The power centers of an organization cling tenaciously to the status quo. Because reengineering is likely to challenge the basis

**Table 6.1**   Causes of Reengineering Failure

- Lack of understanding about reengineering
- Inadequate management of resistance
- Attempting "painless" reengineering
- Too narrow/too broad in scope
- Tepid executive commitment
- Consensus-based approval for reengineering
- Ignoring cultural impediments
- Focusing solely on process redesign
- Responsiblity/authority mismatch
- Ignoring infrastructure alignment
- Calling something else "reengineering"
- Pursuing evolutionary revolution
- Delaying IT enabling role
- Feigning resource commitment
- Caving in to "culture carriers"
- Lack of political critical mass
- The middle management "death zone"
- Lack of courage

for this power, resistance is fierce. Senior management finds itself in a battle between its past and its future. This often results in a delayed or ambiguous response, causing doubt among those who would otherwise support the reengineering effort.

## Attempting "Painless" Reengineering

It is impossible to bring about major change without someone feeling a sense of loss. New processes trigger a number of other changes that will affect many in the organization. The best response is to present the case to justify the need for reengineering and help people make the adjustment. They deserve to hear the truth and be treated as adults.

## Too Narrow/Too Broad in Scope

Trying to reengineer within a function or restrict a team to a single business process serves to marginalize the effort. On the other hand, pursuing too many processes at once will overextend resources and take attention away from critical targets.

## Tepid Executive Commitment

If the senior executive team is unprepared to offer visible and sustained support for reengineering, it will fail.

*If the senior executive team is unprepared to offer visible and sustained support for reengineering, it will fail.*

### Consensus-Based Approval for Reengineering

It is unrealistic to expect to gain a consensus for the scope of change reengineering brings. This is a decision that top management must make.

### Ignoring Cultural Impediments

An organization will find reengineering nearly impossible if it has been unable to set a future direction, is rife with political in-fighting, has allowed an entitlement mentality to emerge among its employees, or requires unanimity before moving forward.

### Focusing Solely on Process Redesign

The success of reengineering requires that the organization realign its infrastructure to support the redesigned processes. Otherwise, it runs the risk of being perceived as hypocritical by calling for major change but continuing to support the status quo.

### Responsibility/Authority Mismatch

One cannot expect a reengineering effort to succeed if its leaders lack the responsibility and authority to cross functional lines. These "ego fortresses" are formidable. This is why core process owners tend to be senior-level executives, most often with profit-and-loss responsibility. When assembling the governing structure, one organization inadvertantly replicated their current hierarchy, not realizing that this choice was likely to suboptimize the search for radical options. It is difficult to juggle the authority granted to pursue current work responsibilities and the authority to overhaul the manner in which this work is performed.

### Ignoring Infrastructure Alignment

People look for signs that a proposed change is going to last. These signs include who gets hired and promoted, what gets measured, how resources are deployed, and what happens to those who take a risk in supporting the change. These activities don't occur without a significant commitment from the organization.

### Calling Something Else "Reengineering"

You can't expect dramatic change from approaches that lack the characteristics found within reengineering. Labeling modest attempts at change as "reengineering" won't do it.

### Pursuing Evolutionary Revolution

The element of time is critical in reengineering. Trying to seek rapid and radical change in a moderate manner is a contradiction in logic. It may reflect confusion of reengineering with a continuous quality improvement effort.

## Delaying IT Enabling Role

Redesign teams need to bring the enabling power of information technology to the table at the start of their reengineering effort. This encourages solutions to support designs that might not otherwise be considered.

## Feigning Resource Commitment

The ceiling of reengineering success is defined by the quality and quantity of resources allocated to the effort. By allowing the urgent to drive out the important, many organizations pull back the resources they have committed, and the result is failure.

## Caving in to "Culture Carriers"

For those who have become comfortable with the status quo, there will always be more reasons for resisting change than accepting it. Putting these people in charge of a reengineering effort is a death sentence for the effort.

## Lack of Political Critical Mass

Even the most powerful senior executive cannot succeed at reengineering without gaining the support of others. Garnering support requires "selling" and "educating" to persuade other executives to stand behind this effort.

## The Middle Management "Death Zone"

Reengineering poses a greater threat to middle management than any other group. This group, by nature of its position in the organization, has the potential to derail a reengineering effort. Senior leadership will need to monitor this resistance closely and take action to overcome it.

## Lack of Courage

More than any other potential pitfalls, the failure of reengineering can be traced to one single source: lack of courage. A senior executive must be willing to commit the organization to this course and take all actions necessary to ensure that it is pursued and supported by the organization. In times of significant change, this takes incredible courage and persistence. It eludes those who refuse to act unless guaranteed of the support of others. We will return to a discussion of leadership of change in Chapter 7.

## A Reality "Checklist"

Some years ago I was having a discussion with a senior vice president about how change occurred in his organization. He said, "We all hold our breath when the CEO returns from vacation. He either has read the most recent management book or else has torn a page out of the airline magazine that touts the latest management fad. Either way, we wind up trying to figure out how to show support for the 'new direction.' After the executive team feigns interest and promises phantom resources for about three months, everything goes back to normal."

Reengineering requires a strong base of support to succeed. Too often, however, the need for support is overlooked by zealots whose fervor obscures the need to win enough converts to pull off the effort. To avoid finding yourself leading a parade of one you need a reality check within the organization. Figure 6.2 is a checklist that can be used to assess whether an organization is ready for reengineering.[7]

The readiness checklist can be used to determine how much support there is for a significant shift in direction. There are several ways to do this. You can route copies of the checklist to key people and seek anonymous responses to use as background for subsequent management discussions. Another option is to ask senior managers to use this as a discussion guide with their direct reports and bring the results back to an executive discussion on reengineering. Yet another approach is to use the checklist as the basis for a formal agenda to discuss the merits of reengineering at the senior level. Generally speaking, the results will support one of the following three actions:

- Weaknesses in most of the organizational dimensions exist and will cause a reengineering effort to fail. The issues raised should be addressed before pursuing reengineering.

- Several organizational dimensions appear weak and could hinder a reengineering effort. Each should be examined and managed closely throughout the effort.

- The results indicate that a reengineering effort will be supported, according to the responses to these organizational dimensions. It would be prudent to validate this more broadly within the organization before proceeding.[8]

These insights may lead to the risk of censure from those who would prefer to avoid the confrontations that result from open dialogue. A less attractive alternative would be to resort to a

**Figure 6.2**   Reengineering Readiness Checklist

—Cost reduction is a major driver for change because our current performance does not yet differentiate our products and services in the marketplace.

—The organization cannot wait for incremental improvements to close the gap between current performance and market expectations.

—There is no understanding of reengineering or a willingness to learn about it at the executive level.

—There is acceptance that reengineering requires top-down direction, and the senior managers are prepared to play the roles to do this.

—It is accepted that new business processes may require skills that exceed those of current employees—even with training.

—The organization is willing to redesign and upgrade its information systems to support future business objectives.

—Our current organization structure helps us make decisions in a timely manner.

—Our departments have individual strategies that are linked to the broader organizational strategy.

—Employees at lower levels have a sufficient degree of trust in the senior management to support a reengineering effort.

—There are "organization change" people who can be assigned to support the reengineering effort (e.g., human resources, organization development, management engineering).

unilateral pronouncement by the senior executive along such lines as this:

> *Yesterday we stood on the edge of a great abyss—*
> *Today we are taking a great leap forward.*

## SUMMARY ···········

A health care organization that chooses reengineering will need to go beyond understanding the technical aspects of the approach. The organizational commitment required is the true price of admission, and a number of issues will need a direct response from senior management and others intent on ensuring success. Senior management will need to gain sufficient knowledge about reengineering to know how to link it to the organization's strategy, and they'll need to demonstrate support for it through periods of significant turbulence. They will also need to prepare and protect those who are involved.

The failure rate of past reengineering efforts is not a mystery. The pitfalls are known and have already been documented by organizations that underestimated what it takes to reengineer core processes. Although there are numerous reasons for such outcomes, the primary cause is a lack of courage among leaders who cannot bring themselves to stay the course in the face of broad resistance from their organizations.

## Notes

1. In their book, *Improving Performance* (San Francisco, Jossey-Bass), G. A. Rummler and A. P. Brache, 1990, discuss how to view performance from an organizational, functional, and individual perspective.

2. For a detailed discussion of the importance of executive involvement in reengineering, see D. Arnoudse, V. DiBianca, and M. Milleman, 1994, "Executive Team Alignment: The Unifying Force in Reengineering," *Insights Quarterly* (Spring): 50–61.

3. This quote is attributed to R. L. Stark of Hallmark Cards, Inc., in M. Hammer and J. Champy, 1993, *Reengineering the Corporation* (New York: Harper Business).

4. Hammer and Champy (see note 3) allude to the higher figure, but a CSC Index, Inc. survey of 621 companies reported a 25 percent failure rate in reengineering, according to *The Wall Street Journal*, 30 June 1994.

5. For those who would like to know more about the businesses cited as experiencing reengineering failure, see B. Caldwell, 1994, "Missteps, Miscues," *InformationWeek*, 20 June; R. C. Copple, 1993, "Patient Care Redesign Process, Budget Neutrality Analysis, and Results," *1993 HIMSS Conference Proceedings*: 243–54; J. Moad, 1994, "Reengineering: Report from the Trenches," *Datamation* (15 March): 36–40; and L. Slavin and B. McWilliams, 1994, "Design for a New Beginning," *Enterprise* (January): 15–17.

6. Other sources have offered advice in this area as well. In addition to the book by Hammer and Champy (see note 3), the Boston Consulting Group published an insightful paper titled "Reengineering and Beyond" in 1993.

7. This checklist is a subset of items from a reengineering readiness survey created by Performance Innovation, Inc., a Dallas-based reengineering consulting business.

8. Recently I came across a description of how *not* to discuss the planning of reengineering: M. Schrage, 1994, "How to Take the Organizational Temperature," *The Wall Street Journal*, 7 November. It seems that a chief executive of a manufacturing conducted a "town meeting" on his company's global computer network.

Everyone had access and their inquiries and responses were anonymous. Shocked executives found that questions about budget cuts were more explicit than they preferred and refused to answer. Unpopular managers were attacked. The CEO pulled the plug after two days, leaving the distinct impression that this was an organization that punished honesty. To paraphrase Hume, truth arises from disagreements among friends. It is necessary to plan more effectively to discern areas of deep concern. Otherwise, "on-line anarchy" will simply wind up being a "whine and geez" session.

## CHAPTER 7

# Change Management

*Machiavelli was an optimist.*

A reengineering "veteran"

**T**HE BUILDING material used to create a bridge, from where an organization is to where it needs to be, consists of the careers of individuals who dare to challenge the status quo. This chilling portrayal is merely an updated version of one given nearly 500 years ago:

> It must be remembered that there is nothing more difficult to plan, more doubtful of success, nor more dangerous to manage, than the creation of a new system. For the initiator has the enmity of all who would profit by preservation of the old institution and merely lukewarm defenders in those who would gain by the new ones.
> —*Niccolo Machiavelli, 1513*

The magnitude of change needed to justify the application of reengineering is matched only by the magnitude of change it then creates within an organization. This chapter examines how to embed change management within a reengineering effort. It offers insights into the points of leverage that can be used to gain support for reengineering and ensure successful implementation of redesigned processes. This includes understanding the frame of mind of those who introduce change, those who resist change, and those who are caught in the middle.

## BRINGING HOME HEALTH CARE REENGINEERING

It has become almost a truism in the business community that top-level executives bring "home" change initiatives that subsequently receive less than universal endorsement from their organizations. Reengineering, is certainly no exception (see Figure 7.1). While we would hope that senior managers would not make a decision to reengineer without the steps we have discussed earlier, it is quite likely that even the "right" decision will face enormous challenge in the organization. Top management commitment is essential, yet few managers have had the experience of trying to bring about significant change in the face of almost certain resistance throughout an organization. Many of them, upon encountering such a reaction, retreat and attempt to pursue change in a less obtrusive manner. Managers in the health care industry would be poorly advised to take this path. Instead, they must try to understand the dynamics of change and use this knowledge to help sustain the effort. Unfortunately, many senior managers believe what they are experiencing is unique and that no historic precedents exist to guide them.

*Few managers have had the experience of trying to bring about significant change in the face of almost certain resistance.*

## A MISGUIDED THEORY OF CHANGE

There are several business myths that are remarkably resistant to attempts to set the record straight. We have all heard such aphorisms as, "A happy worker is a productive worker," and "If it is worth doing, it is worth doing well," and "Work hard and your career will take care of itself."

**Figure 7.1**  The CEO Brings Home Reengineering

Within the framework of change management lies a myth that has resulted in the waste of innumerable resources, not to mention lost opportunities in the marketplace. The following quote sums up this misperception:

> Most change programs don't work because they are guided by a theory of change that is fundamentally flawed. The common belief is that the place to begin is with the knowledge and attitudes of individuals. Changes in attitudes, the theory goes, lead to changes in individual behavior.[1]

Anyone who can remember the introduction of Civil Rights legislation in the 1960s might recall a statement that served as the core principle behind it: You cannot legislate morality—only behavior. The assumption was that attitudes and beliefs are likely to be influenced by a change in behavior. Reengineering is based on changing work processes, thus leading to required changes in behavior. Rather than building teams that are peripheral to the business context, reengineering calls for teams to address specific core processes, thus setting the stage for environmental reconfiguration that will almost certainly lead to changes in the way people think and feel about their work. In short, reengineering looks to change attitudes through changes in behavior.

## DIMENSIONS OF CHANGE

The organizational change model presented in Chapter 2 reflects insights gained from over a quarter of a century of management research. At the center of the model are four key dimensions: leadership, workforce, structure, and process. It is most unfortunate that organizations have attempted to bring about change by focusing on only one or two of these dimensions—at the expense of the others. Several of the reengineering failures discussed in Chapter 6 fell into this trap, and failure is the likely result when the organization does not comprehend its current state of readiness for change.

Among the activities within the *process diagnosis* step of process reengineering is determining change readiness (see Figure 4.6). Change readiness is related to reengineering readiness, but it takes a closer look at the four dimensions in terms of current management practices. Conducting a candid assessment of an organization's readiness for change is a telling part of the overall change process. It helps to "unfreeze" current thinking about how the organization operates and to determine what challenges lie ahead in the effort to bring about change. It is like holding up a mirror to the organization to see what it looks like in the eyes of various stakeholders.

A variety of approaches can be used to assess readiness, including a review of past change history, customer and stakeholder interviews, and a survey of organizational members. Often this helps to reveal patterns that help to guide the organization through its change efforts.

Throughout the book we have focused predominantly on the dimensions of process and structure. It is helpful to balance this with some insights about the remaining two dimensions: leadership and workforce. Let us begin by examining the characteristics of people who have led successful change.

## · · · · · · · · · · LEADERS OF CHANGE

There has been a significant amount of research into the relationship between leadership and successful change.[2] As one considers the leadership attributes that recur in examples of successful change, the ones that occur most frequently include the following:

- **Provide own recognition/reward:** Successful change leaders rely less often on others as their source of reward and recognition. This allows them the freedom to make decisions without plebiscites. Within a reengineering effort, this is critical because the potential outcomes will not be as apparent to others for some time. As someone once said, "I'll see it when I believe it."

- **Courage from deeply held values:** Leaders' values and beliefs often cause others grief because they are articulated without regard to the protection of myths or the status quo. In many cases, these leaders find it difficult to articulate the basis for their actions and they appear to be purely intuitive. In reality, they have been shaped by experiences and lessons learned over a long period of time.

- **Near-irrational hatred of inaction:** Change leaders would easily agree with the statement that inaction speaks louder than words. They are convinced that they must use tools like information, resources, and support to take advantage of change.

- **Empowerment as means to end:** Successful leaders of change believe in building environments that allow people to grow and rise to their own levels of capability. Some people mistake their endorsement of empowerment as being driven by humanitarian concerns. More often they choose this path as the most direct route to bring about a new order of things.

- **Thrive within sustained ambiguity:** Change leaders revel in the fragments of order around them and take great pleasure in bringing order out of chaos. To do this, they find it necessary to "dumb the complexity down" to its basic elements. This allows them to see opportunities when others see only pandemonium.

- **Bureaucracies are anathema to them:** To supporters of the status quo, change leaders appear to demonstrate ingratitude for the benefits gained from their organizations in the past. In truth, they find themselves having to destroy the systems they once supported. This is the key to creating new work environments that offer a better balance between patriarchal dependency and entrepreneurial autonomy.

Occasionally it is possible to find an expression of change leadership in the behaviors and words these individuals use to express themselves. Compare, for example, the following two leaders. In a large health insurance company, the senior executive had a reputation for extreme caution. As the health care reform debate grew in intensity, he routed around an article talking about changes occurring in other industries, adding these words in his note: "Many believe we are about to experience similar or greater change." Many who read this wondered what the executive *himself* believed. Contrast the tone of his words with those of Ronald E. Compton, the CEO of Aetna, about what it takes to bring about significant change: "Change is not something that happens. It's a way of life. It's not a process, it's a value. It's not something you do, it engulfs you."[3]

The leadership dimension cannot be ignored by those pursuing reengineering. Unless you have the level of dedication expressed by Aetna's CEO, you will fight rear guard action indefinitely. Ultimately, leaders draw their strength from those willing to be led. The need to gain their commitment comes at a time when they may be questioning their relationship with their organization.

## THE CHANGING WORKFORCE CONTRACT

Reengineering will bring about changes in the nature of work that will in turn raise significant questions about the quid pro quo regarding employment agreements.[4] The workforce is affected by any change in the psychological employment contract between employee and employer. Table 7.1 shows some of the key elements that are changing within this contract.

People are beginning to reassess the basis for their commitment and the degree to which they will allow the organization to define their worth. Consider these implications:

- People believe their positions are "written in pencil" and avoid organizational efforts to lock them into one of powerlessness. This reflects a significant shift in thinking from lifelong employment to lifelong employability.
- The destruction of career paths and the flattening of organizations has resulted in people seeking more relevant recognition of their accomplishments.
- Involvement with accountability is the currency of the realm. The working climate is moving from command and control to voice and choice.
- Loyalty is demonstrated through contribution, not necessarily through longevity. Departures are being celebrated—networks transcending employers are in.
- Open acknowledgment of "temporariness" is more common. Emphasis on valuing diversity is based in part on appreciating the worth and breadth of external experience.

The underlying theme here is the shift in power. The most democratic source of power is knowledge. The fragmenting of processes is paralleled by the fragmenting of knowledge. Reengineering moves knowledge to where it can be used most effectively. Gaining the commitment and full potential of the workforce will require reuniting process and knowledge. This was expressed quite eloquently by Alvin Toffler:

**Table 7.1**
Old and New Employment Contracts

| Old Contract | New Contract |
| --- | --- |
| • Long-term employment | • Situational relationship |
| • Reward for performance is promotion | • Reward for performance is sense of relevance/contribution |
| • Paternalistic management | • Empowering management |
| • Loyalty = staying | • Loyalty = good work |
| • Implicit lifetime career | • Explicit job contracting |

...in every bureaucracy, knowledge is broken apart horizontally and put back together vertically. Any serious restructure of business or government must directly attack the organization of knowledge.[5]

In a changing working environment that comes to emphasize flexibility and adaptability, many organizations have sought to achieve optimal physical resource management through so-called virtual offices. The concept of a permanent physical space is being replaced by temporary workplace assignments that exist in computer memory. An employee arrives and is assigned to a space with a phone jack, electrical outlet, and an illuminated flat surface. Now organizations are even having to contend with the emergence of "virtual employees" who only exist when *they* are turned on.

## EMBEDDING CHANGE MANAGEMENT IN REENGINEERING

The business reengineering model in Chapter 4 showed how an organization wraps itself around a reengineering effort (see Figure 4.2). The components of the model rest upon the management of change, which reengineering experts view as a critical ingredient to success.

It is important not to view change management as separate from the model. Although the change management literature has produced numerous insights into this area over the past few years, a common error is to pursue change management outside of a specific context or set of organizational objectives. In short, change management often comes to be treated as a generic fix that requires only moderate understanding of any given organization's uniqueness. For that reason, the relationship between change management and reengineering needs to be clear.

Figure 7.2 shows how the key components of change management are embedded within the business reengineering model:

- **Fear leads to vision:** With some significant exceptions, the overwhelming majority of examples of organization change are precipitated by fear. This fear serves to move an organization to reexamine its future—an activity found within the development of the process structure component. Recall that the process design teams pursue a vision of their own efforts as well.

- **Change champions:** The need to identify and position change champions forms the basis for the establishment of a governing structure and the selection of process design teams.

- **New behavior leads to new attitudes:** A change in environment leads to a change in behavior, thus bringing about attitude change. The process design teams will seek redesign options within the process reengineering component.

- **Change levers:** The change management literature discusses "change levers" that can be used to help sustain and reinforce the change being sought. The attempt to align the organizational infrastructure draws heavily upon these levers. An example of this leverage will be discussed later.

- **Model new environment:** The role of information technology as an enabler of reengineering change includes the creation of prototypes of the future environment. This occurs when technical solutions are integrated into process redesign.

- **Continuous learning:** Finally, the concept of continuous learning is at the heart of continuous improvement; this knowledge is used to enhance the gains from re-engineering.

## APPLYING CHANGE LEVERS

People look for signs of an organization's commitment to change. The form and content of communication is one sign. Symbolic

**Figure 7.2** Change Management Embedded within Business Reengineering Model

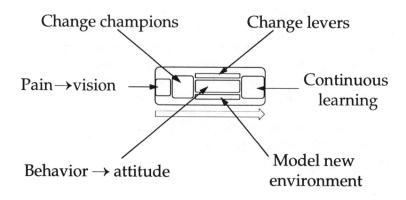

acts may be another. But there are other signs that are so common
that they are often overlooked:

- The kind of people hired
- The responsibilities within jobs
- The position of a job within a structure
- The movement of people into positions of authority
- How performance is defined, monitored, and rewarded
- The opportunities for growth and advancement
- The content stressed in training and development activity.

Taken separately, these may not appear particularly powerful,
but as a set, they represent the most powerful levers of change
that exist within an organization.

In Chapter 4 we discussed the need to align the organizational
infrastructure to redesigned processes. The "change levers" we have
listed above constitute an organization's capacity to influence the
change process through its use of "people systems." Figure 7.3 offers
a Strategic Human Asset Model that helps convey the systemic
nature of these levers.[6]

In the upper left corner, the impetus for change is the business
strategy. Within a reengineering context, this often takes the
form of process team recommendations to modify or develop

**Figure 7.3** Strategic Human Asset Model

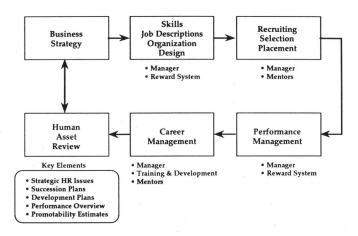

*Source:* The Change Riders: Managing the Power of Change *(pp. 127 and
259), © 1991 by G. D. Kissler. Reprinted by permission of Addison-Wesley
Publishing Company, Inc.*

ure to support process redesign. From this point
the model clockwise. To support the redesign,
e identified and grouped into new positions. These
designed structures—most likely horizontal—and
rnal and external) is assessed for purposes of
ople are located, selected, and placed in the new
rmance management process allows individuals
to set goals, receive feedback, and gain organizational
recognition. Paths for career growth more often move laterally,
versus climbing a functional promotional ladder. In addition, an
organization would offer training and job opportunities to help
encourage professional growth.

Finally, a review of the "value" of the people currently
supporting the organization takes place. The information gained
through such activities as succession planning, development needs,
and promotability estimates, are used to guide subsequent business
strategy.

Organizations that attempt significant change find that they
must take control of this process. This often results in a significant
debate over who "owns" the process. A human resources function
can design, develop, and support it, but it really belongs to the
organization's managers.[7] The power of these levers of change
must be put in the hands of those with the responsibility and
accountability for determining and implementing business strategy.
The most likely candidates are those who serve in a general
management position with profit and loss responsibility. The most
successful change management approaches combine this ownership
with the support and counsel of human resources professionals.

## THE ESSENCE OF CHANGE MANAGEMENT

One of the more surprising outcomes from reengineering is
a decrease in organizational performance—initially. Despite the
claims of zealots promoting alternatives to reengineering, this
occurs when *any* significant effort is made to introduce change.
There are several reasons for this. Some are benign (e.g., people
need time to get comfortable with new performance expectations),
and others result from resistance to change.

Figure 7.4 offers an interesting display of the relationship
between the phenomenon of reduced performance resulting from
change and steps required to overcome resistance to change.
The lower portion is called a "change curve." The curve shows
the normal performance prior to introducing large-scale change,

followed by a decline labeled as the "Valley of Despair," followed by a new level of performance. The "Valley of Despair" gets its name from the organization's typical reaction to the decrease in performance. Many managers recoil in horror and try to back out of the effort. Most find out, to their chagrin, that the easy way out usually leads back in!

Such a decrease in performance—far from being an unusual outcome—is to be expected. The valley does not signal a failed strategy; it just calls attention to the need for change management activities that minimize the downturn. The essence of change management is minimizing the breadth and depth of this downturn. Not *eliminating* it—just minimizing it. To understand this challenge, one has to examine the forms of resistance an organization is likely to encounter during a reengineering effort. Figure 7.5 offers insight into three types of resistance: technical, political, and cultural.[8]

### Technical Resistance

Technical resistance is the most rational form of resistance and reflects concerns one would expect from those who assess the impact of change in terms of cost, resource constraints, preparation, and available skills. Within a health care organization, the issues most likely to occur in this category are the following:

- **Sunk costs:** There is an inverse relationship between the amount of capital investments required (the cost of

**Figure 7.4** The Essence of Change Management

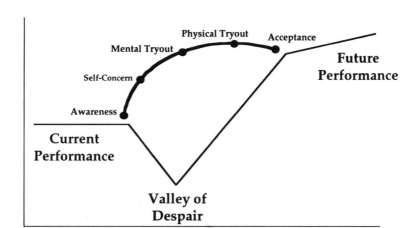

**Figure 7.5** Source of Reengineering Resistance

**Technical**

- Devalued knowledge/skills
- "Sunk cost"
- Loss or lack of expertise
- Lack of support systems
- Resource limitations
- Programmed behavior

**Cultural**

- Lack of trust
- Fear of public failure
- Competing values/philosophies
- Threatened job security
- Passive aggression
- Technophobia
- Organization inertia
- Expectations of autonomy
- Unofficial restraints

**Political**

- Shift in influence, authority, and control
- Loss of social status
- Resource allocation
- Official restraints
- Organization agreements

acquiring new knowledge or skills) and an organization's willingness to undergo change.

- **Resource limitations:** The power to change requires resources, and many health care organizations are severely constrained as it is. Under these circumstances, one will find an argument made for adhering to low-demand routines and behaviors. The prospect of loss of market share, marginal facilities, and regulatory pressure serve to strengthen this argument.

- **Programmed behavior:** We have discussed the power of infrastructure to support change. The reverse is also true. In environments with highly proscribed roles and responsibilities, the people systems (e.g., selection, rewards, training) work to sustain this environment. This results in a form of "tunnel vision" on the part of people who have lost sight of broader opportunities for change because they are so dedicated to their specialty areas.

## Political Resistance

This is the area where power and influence reign. The arguments based on politics will stem from the fear of loss of power, status, influence, and sense of self-worth. Health care organizations find certain political arguments particularly common:

- **Official constraints on behavior:** Internal policies, coupled with external statutes and regulations, serve to constrain the support for change.
- **Interorganizational agreements:** In an environment that has invested heavily in commitments to share equipment and facilities, form alliances, agree to mergers, and integrate staffs, these serve as buffers to change.

## Cultural Resistance

Someone once said that it's hard to fight an enemy with outposts in your head. This is the less rational side of resistance. Fear, lack of trust, inertia, and conflicting values all serve to create barriers to change. The health care environment typically finds this resistance taking these forms:

- **Stability rapture:** Predictability becomes a reward for resisting change. The predisposition to resist change generally arises from a fear of loss of control over one's life. The result is a viewpoint that the status quo is "reality" and beyond question.
- **Autonomy über alles:** Mix the ingredients of specialized skills and critical work and you have a heady brew. Health care professionals, particularly physicians, have come to expect a high degree of autonomy. Any change that threatens this will be resisted at nearly any cost.
- **Unofficial constraints:** The informal organizations within health institutions wield significant power, particularly when composed of high-status health professionals, including physicians. One need only examine the overlapping committee structures, patterns of referrals, and associations with external sources of technical support to recognize the ties that bind physicians to historic patterns of medical care delivery.
- **Calculated opposition:** Far from being a casual sense of discomfort, this resistance is focused and intense, and is driven by concerns for lost prestige and a lowering of quality in health care delivery.

Creating lists of reasons to resist change does not deserve a standing ovation. There are no prizes for predicting rain—only for building arks. In this spirit, we return to the upper portion of Figure 7.5, which displays a series of steps that can be taken to help "fence sitters" embrace change. This array is often called the "acceptance curve."

*There are no prizes for predicting rain—only for building arks.*

The first step helps people become aware of the need for change and how it will be brought about. A focused communication effort is required here. (We will have more to say about the role of communication later.) The next step offers an answer to the inevitable fundamental question, "What's in it for me?" If the organization can provide justification for participation, the likelihood of resistance diminishes.

Just as athletes mentally prepare themselves for competitive events, people need to mentally rehearse for the change and its potential impact on them. The development of a vision will be quite helpful here. The next step involves an actual hands-on experience with the change. This can come with exposure to prototypes, training opportunities, and visits to sites where the proposed change is in operation.

Don't be misled by the linear nature of this curve. Experience shows many examples of "backsliding" before people come to the final stage of acceptance. Of course, we are focusing here on people who have legitimate concerns about change and who deserve management's attention. Later we will discuss those whose resistance is "hard-wired" and what can be done to address it.

## COMMUNICATION: ANTIDOTE TO STEALTH REENGINEERING

A few years ago I was addressing an audience in Ireland made up of senior executives of a company facing a rapidly changing international market. Their organization had a long history of intransigence and inefficiency, and many doubted it was possible to change the behaviors so deeply ingrained in the workforce. When I offered one of change management's prime maxims— "No change without pain"—it was clear that these words caused some discomfort for several audience members. At one point an individual asked, "What if there is no pain?" I answered, "Inflict it." Another shot back, "You mean to say you recommend causing deliberate pain?!" "Yes," I answered, "the pain of awareness."

In a similar situation, a health care organization that was facing the need for dramatic change continued to project exactly the opposite perception in its communication to employees and the public. The newsletters, videotapes, and public appearances all sent the same message: "Everything is fine. We are doing very well, indeed. Don't worry." Of course, the employees knew otherwise. The top management team failed to recognized that the staff was bright enough and informed enough to figure out what was happening. The disparity between the internal and external messages was so obvious that it made the executives appear either ignorant or deceptive.

As the situation grew more grave, the senior executive finally spoke openly to his direct reports about the need for a radical improvement in performance—particularly their cost structure. The picture he painted was radical. A very small subset of the executive group began to plan a reengineering effort. Unfortunately, the cultural precedent of obscuring bad news continued. The reengineering plans were laid, the overall approach was developed, and the entire effort was kept under wraps from all but one or two people.

The senior executive overseeing the development of the reengineering approach finally broached the subject in a meeting with other executives. Two issues became quite apparent. First, his knowledge of reengineering was nominal and therefore he found it difficult to explain any but the broadest aspects of the approach. Second, he had not shared this information with the others in any significant detail prior to the meeting. The result was sadly predictable. Those who had been working on the reengineering method, tools, and training had argued unsuccessfully for a more direct and open form of communication. When this was rejected, they began to refer to the approach as "stealth reengineering."

Change management begins by framing the need for change and sharing it with those affected. It is surprising how many organizations handle communication in an abysmal manner. Once, when someone confronted a senior team with this accusation, one of them replied, "We don't have a communication problem; we just don't know what to say."

## The Keys to Successful Communication

Change management is so closely linked with effective communication that it is surprising how often it is ignored. Research has shown, for example, that only 44 percent of companies that downsized between 1990 and 1995 shared details of their plans—only 34 percent bothered to communicate to the "survivors." Pursuing reengineering means accepting a simple fact: the odds of gaining support for the change increase with the advent of effective communication plans.

There are at least four key communication issues that need to be addressed: credible source, case for action, change process, and self-interest.

- **Credible source:** Communication success depends heavily on choosing a believable spokesperson—there is no sense having a critical message delivered by someone the organization will ignore. In most instances, this calls for the senior manager or CEO to play the role.

- **Case for action:** We have emphasized elsewhere the need for a credible, candid, and well-documented case for action. This should be an intelligent message for adults. We have seen well-produced videos that give no hint of the true anticipated magnitude of change—leading to resentment by those who later believe they were misled.

- **Change process:** The approach the organization will follow to bring about change must be introduced, explained, and connected to the future view of the business. Some of the critical questions that will be asked over various stages of a reengineering effort include:

  — What is health care reengineering?
  — Why are we doing it?
  — Who will be affected?
  — How long will it last?
  — How will we know we are done?
  — Who will be left?

- **Self-interest:** Ultimately, the organization must help each individual answer the question, "What's in it for me?" There is no ducking this, and efforts to avoid it only increase the likelihood of resistance.

It is ironic that some of the organizations that are held up as having succeeded at reengineering are very critical of their own communication efforts. This is an insight that others considering reengineering should not ignore.

## The Mechanics of Communication

I have come to have great respect for people who understand the power and nuances of communication. The management of change resembles a political campaign, and few would deny the impact that communication has had in politics.

The development of a strategic communication plan is a critical activity within a reengineering effort. The plan should be formulated by the reengineering leadership group for organizationwide use and by redesign teams that focus on changes related to a specific core process. We cannot do justice to a full description of such plans here, but among the issues that such campaigns take very seriously are these:

- **Target audience:** The research on audience selection is an interesting blend of art and science—this often is reflected in terms such as "demographics" and "psychographics."

- **Tailored message:** Audience selection leads inexorably to decisions on what needs to be communicated and how this message needs to "sound" to the audience. In short, content is as critical as tone.

- **Multimedia:** Our society has come to expect information from numerous sources. Ignoring this can result in significant portions of an audience not receiving the message because the medium chosen was not one they prefer. The choice of medium not only is important because of who attends to it, it is important because it represents a portion of the message itself.

- **Timing/frequency:** During times of change, people go through various stages of receptiveness to communicated messages. It is very difficult to predict when a message will be accepted, so effective communication includes planned redundancy as well as deliberate use of events as vehicles to help carry the message. The "Rule of 50" says—somewhat tongue-in-cheek—that you need to say something 50 times before people believe it.

- **Prepare messengers:** Communication experts will tell you that most people believe they communicate well—and they don't. It is essential that people who accept the responsibility for communication receive coaching on how to be more effective communicators.

- **Monitor reaction:** Those who have lived through communication efforts will tell you they benefited from feedback to help shape the delivery and content of messages. Employees never complain about receiving too much communication.

## THINGS THEY WON'T TEACH IN SCHOOL

There are several issues in change management that are not often discussed—most likely out of concern for being "politically correct." Let us risk censure by pointing out a few:

### Authoritarian Democracy

Someone has to say to the organization, "We are going to climb the mountain on the left. Just how we climb it is up for debate.

But make no mistake about which one it is. End of discussion." Those who feel queasy about how this might be interpreted as something less than participative have legitimate fears. Few large-scale change efforts begin by consensus. Rather, one often finds a single driven individual who insists it be done (take Boris Yeltsin, for example).

## Forced Exit

We discussed earlier how to overcome normal resistance. Now we come to the die-hards whose heads are "hard-wired." Their resistance to reengineering is nothing short of a threat to the organization, and they should be removed from positions where their influence can undermine the reengineering effort. This often includes persuading them to "flourish elsewhere" because they will never buy into the new management philosophy and working environment. This is a particularly difficult, albeit small, group to deal with. They are out of touch and tend to escape reality on the horse of rhetoric.

## Solution Becomes the Problem

One phenomenon that surprises many rational managers is that the harder they push on the organization, the harder it pushes back! They mistakenly assume that resistance can be overcome simply by communicating. To their chagrin they find that better-informed people use this knowledge to increase their attacks on the "problem"—meaning the change process, or reengineering itself. This calls for a review of the change levers available. As grandma used to say, "Don't try to talk yourself out of a problem you behaved yourself into."

## Commitment/Compliance Illusion

One of the most perplexing issues is "feigned compliance" served up in the form of fervid verbal commitment to the change process. Nothing short of behavioral demonstrations of commitment should be used as criteria to judge whether there has been significant buy-in in the organization. This is particularly true at the executive level, although the literature accurately describes a fair bit of this occurring among middle management as well. Don't confuse conformity with unity or agreement.

## REENGINEERING: ON THE ROAD TO...?

Changes in performance come about through changes in behavior. Seeking changes in attitudes, in hopes of subsequent changes in behavior, is a fool's errand. Yet it is amazing how often this occurs. A group finds it is dysfunctional and prescribes "team-building" as a solution. They all go out and play golf. They come back and find themselves—dysfunctional. Of course. Learning to interact more effectively on a golf course has practically nothing to do with what the group will face on the next day back at work.

This is a significant lesson for those who think the first order of business in reengineering is empowerment or involvement. Reengineering demands that people focus on the work itself, assuming that most problems have less to do with the people than with how they are asked to work. If you pit a good performer against a bad system, the system will win almost every time. We spend too much of our time "fixing" people who are not broken, and not enough time fixing organization systems that are.

*If you pit a good performer against a bad system, the system will win almost every time.*

But what about negative behavior? Some would have us think this is a "spirituality" issue. They believe one should pursue higher-order goals of morality and that this leads naturally to a more pleasant environment. There is certainly room for philosophical debate over what a "healthy" society should value. But remember the discussion between the father of Eliza Doolittle and Professor Higgins in "My Fair Lady"? Professor Higgins asks Eliza's father if he has no morals. Her father replies that he can't afford them. Most negative behavior in organizations has far less to do with an absence of human sensitivity than it does with having to contend with a dysfunctional environment on a daily basis. Reengineering is aimed at this dysfunction.

On the other hand, people do come to appreciate stability and a predictable work environment—even if it is largely dysfunctional in the broader organizational perspective. In such cases, the changes being sought through reengineering will not receive thunderous applause. In fact, many people will see the immediate changes in a negative light and will need to pass through this period before they appreciate fully the benefits of reengineering. Table 7.2 portrays two views of the outcomes of reengineering. We should hardly expect the disruptions from reengineering to be viewed without regret by many in the organization. Frankly, for many, the road to nirvana passes through nervosa, a psychological state of agitation.

For those who believe in the need to gain commitment through empowerment and in removing unnecessary hand-offs between levels of management, the reengineering road leads to redistributed power. Those who regard such structure and direction as essential will see the arrival of anarchy. The fact is that we are witnessing the end of the Industrial Revolution and, with it, the end

**Table 7.2**
Reengineering
Outcomes

| Nirvana | Nervosa |
| --- | --- |
| Redistributed power | Anarchy |
| "Cognitariat" | Proletariet |
| Pay for contribution | Unemployment |
| Horizontal efficiency | Vertical disintegration |
| Sustainable existence | Performance crisis |
| Increased confidence | Loss of stability |

of macroeconomics as a guide to how to position for international change. Those who would seek meritocracy need to realize that others will regard this as social Darwinism. The "cognitariat" actually will become a class distinction that cannot be breached through arbitrary applications of money or social standing. We need to understand that many people with low capacity for learning or with minimal job skills will face a daunting world that calls for more complex people, more complex jobs, and significantly less complex processes.[9]

*Reengineering is the ultimate form of "hardball" in an organizational setting.*

People who want reward and recognition tied more directly to personal contribution will see reengineering as an idea whose time has come. Others will never view it as anything other than an instrument used to create a loss of jobs. In their eyes, a horizontal focus to gain speed, service, and capacity for learning will be the destruction of a cherished form of predictable and well-defined vertical boundaries. For many, the "loss of tradition" associated with reengineering will stand out as irreplaceable and will never be justified by the positive outcomes otherwise achieved. A careful look at the "change curve" can predict two opposing views of change in performance: one will see the creation of a means to sustain the viability of an organization and its people; others will see nothing but decreased performance. Reengineering is the ultimate form of "hardball" in an organizational setting, and change management is the means of bringing along the critical mass of people needed to ensure its success.

## THE THIRD PARTY

As we consider the reaction of the people in our organizations to reengineering, it is worth remembering that others are also watching our efforts. A union organizer in the health care industry was quoted as saying, "You organize in the face of change because that is what creates uncertainty and that's what we have here."[10] These words should be taken quite seriously. Despite the decrease in union membership throughout the 1980s, there is growing evidence that the organizing strategy is shifting toward the professionals who feel disenfranchised by their "parents" and are showing increased willingness to band together to protect their economic base. Labor analysts estimate that a quarter of the U.S. workforce exists on the fringes of corporations in part-time or temporary positions. Though contract workers may not display the same company loyalty as their full-time colleagues, the advantages are obvious: Companies can increase productivity while providing fewer—or no—benefits.

There is no reason for alarm. For the most part, unions exist because management's gross incompetence has created a need for them. Third-party representation is not needed as long as people believe they have been treated equitably in an adult fashion. Reengineering will bring about major disruption and offers the opportunity for exploitation by those who will seize upon the ambiguity and fear associated with it. Change management offers an opportunity to avoid such possibilities.

## JUST A MATTER OF TIME

Many of you will be charged with the responsibility for helping your organizations move reengineering efforts forward. The necessity for change has been made more than obvious; denying it will lead to very costly delays. It is only a matter of time until the magnitude of change will become apparent—don't wait until it is too late to take the steps necessary to address it.

The material in this book offers a firm basis for justifying and implementing health care reengineering. The details of the purpose, principles, and processes of reengineering should be discussed within organizations to tailor this approach to individual needs. Although it is impossible to anticipate every issue that will come up, this book should help you set the effort in motion. It is better to be roughly right than exactly wrong.

The future of health care is dependent upon something that this book does not and cannot provide: courage. Given the magnitude of change in this industry, reengineering is the approach of choice. Those who pursue it will be among those who emerge stronger and more competitive in the future.

## SUMMARY

Health care reengineering will meet with significant resistance, despite the endorsement it receives from top management. To address this, it is necessary to understand change management and how it fits within a reengineering effort. Reengineering avoids trying to change behavior by first changing attitudes—the cause of most change failure. Instead, it addresses four key dimensions that are critical to a change effort—leadership, workforce, structure, and process—with the expectation that changing behaviors will result in changed attitudes.

Leaders of change have certain characteristics that allow them to encourage the support and commitment of others faced with difficult transitions. Among the most important are the ability to pursue change based on strong convictions and the ability to understand how their own behavior affects the change outcome itself. Today's leaders face a changing psychological contract between employees and the organization. It reflects the growing reality that work relationships are less often permanent, are based on work to be performed, and offer reward for achievement rather than obedience.

The business reengineering model was revisited in this chapter to show how change management is embedded within it. Key change management principles include the need for a vision, changing attitudes through changes in behavior, and applying change levers. Particular attention should be paid to the type and nature of change levers that reflect the "people systems" within an organization.

Change initially produces a reduction in performance, and steps should be taken to reduce—but not avoid—this outcome. The challenge is to identify and address the technical, political, and cultural resistance to change. Among the most powerful ways to address resistance is through the effective use of communication.

Some examples of health care organizations that are pursuing reengineering efforts will be offered in the following chapter.

## Notes

1. For a more detailed discussion of the myths that have derailed change efforts, see M. Beer, R. A. Eisenstat, and B. Spector, 1990. "Why Change Programs Don't Produce Change," *Harvard Business Review* 68 (November–December): 158–65.

2. For some insightful reading on the subject of leadership, I would recommend W. Bennis, 1989, *Why Leaders Can't Lead* (San Francisco: Jossey-Bass); W. Bennis and B. Nanus, 1985, *Leaders* (New York: Harper & Row); J. Champy, 1995, *Reengineering Management* (New York: Harper Business); G. D. Kissler, 1991, *The Change Riders* (Reading, MA: Addison-Wesley); and N. Tichy and M. A. Devanna, 1986, *The Transformational Leader* (New York: John Wiley & Sons).

3. Ron Compton's "Ten Commandments" are quoted in G. Rifkin, 1993, "Reengineering Aetna," *Forbes ASAP* (7 June): 77–86.

4. An unusual opportunity to examine the change in the psychological employment contact is offered in 1994, *Human Resource Management* 33 (Fall). The ideas related to the list of issues within Figure 7.2 are taken from G. D. Kissler, 1994, "The New Employment Contract," *Human Resource Management* 33 (Fall): 335–52. I also recommend J. Bardwick, 1991, *Danger in the Comfort Zone* (New York: AMACOM). It helps explain the need to overcome an entitlement mentality among employees. For further discussion of the emerging shift in these relationships, see the cover story of *Business Week* (17 October 1994): 76–87.

5. I was quite pleased to see the position taken by A. Toffler. It was the first time I had encountered the notion that knowledge, not just processes, had become fragmented across organizations. For more details, see his 1990 book, *PowerShift* (New York: Bantam Books), 172.

6. For a more detailed discussion of this model and its components, see pages 126–55 in *The Change Riders*, cited earlier. The impact (positive or negative) of human resource systems on the development of competencies that support strategic direction is described in A. A. Lado and M. C. Wilson, 1994 "Human Resource Systems and Sustained Competitive Advantage: A Competency-Based Perspective," *The Academy of Management Review* 19 (October): 699–727.

7. A very persuasive case is made for this point in M. Beer, B. Spector, P. R. Lawrence, D. Quinn Mills, and R. E. Walton, 1984, *Managing Human Assets* (New York: The Free Press).

8. The categories of resistance are taken from the work of N. M. Tichy. He has offered a number of examples of how this typology helps to understand the concept of change management. A discussion of this can be found in the book cited earlier, *The Transformational Leader*. Some of the examples of resistance within the health care industry are found in W. R. Boss, 1989, *Organization Development in Health Care* (Reading, MA: Addison-Wesley OD Series).

9. Toffler used the word "cognitariat" to describe the new classification of employee who is expert in the access and use of information. See his book, *PowerShift*, cited earlier. The polarization of people based on skills and the ability to obtain/maintain them is described in M. J. Mandel, 1994, "Business Rolls the Dice," *Business Week* (17 October): 88–90; and in D. Farney, 1994, "Have Liberals Ignored 'Have-Less' Whites at Their Own Peril," *The Wall Street Journal*, 14 December.

10. A discussion of the shift in thinking among health care employees with regard to third-party representation appears in R. Tomsho, 1994, "Mounting Sense of Job Malaise Prompts More Health-Care Workers to Join Unions," *The Wall Street Journal*, 9 June. For an example of how nurses are reacting to work redesign, see L. Kertesz, 1994, "California Nurses File Suit to Stop Work Redesign," *Modern Healthcare* (19 September): 14.

## CHAPTER 8

# Case Studies in Health Care Reengineering

*It works if you do it right.*

A reengineering "czar"

**W**E NOW turn to three case studies to illustrate how reengineering is performed within a health care organization. One is a large teaching hospital, another is a smaller regional hospital, and one is a health care insurer. Both of the hospitals had made significant commitments to the development and implementation of quality programs. In fact, their prior work aided their subsequent reengineering effort to a great degree. However, both organizations recognized that their markets had changed faster than anyone had anticipated. This called for a more dramatic effort to increase performance and an approach that would help meet this goal. In each case, the choice was reengineering. Although there is some variation in how each organization tailored reengineering to fit its needs, the fundamental principles are being applied in both cases.

*Both organizations recognized that their markets had changed faster than anyone had anticipated.*

The application of reengineering in the insurance company offers interesting insights into how the approach can be tailored to the specific needs of a nonhospital health care organization. This organization's reengineering effort was preceded by a sociotechnical systems approach. Although some of the group dynamics experiences were helpful in preparing the organization for reengineering, it was clear that the earlier effort lacked the capability to bring about the rapid and radical change needed.

Pay particular attention to the role technology played *prior* to the formation of reengineering teams.

## METHODIST MEDICAL CENTER

### Background

Methodist Medical Center, part of the Methodist Hospitals of Dallas system in Dallas, Texas, is a 463-bed tertiary teaching and referral hospital. The medical center includes units for organ transplantation, maternity, oncology, neurology, cardiology, trauma, critical care, and other general medical and surgical services. The Methodist Hospitals system and its subsidiaries maintain an employee base of 2,200, with more than 500 physicians on the medical staff.

### Case for Action

The hospital sector of the health care industry is undergoing significant change. Among the many issues they face is the rapid shift from an inpatient to an ambulatory care setting due to clinical and technological advances as well as pressure from insurers. Methodist has witnessed a significant volume of care moving to the outpatient side with 20.2 percent of the system's revenue coming from outpatient services.

Methodist recognized that the volume of care and its capacity to handle this volume were critical success factors that would affect Methodist's strategy to be a community provider of integrated, affordable, and high-quality health care services in the future. One other driving consideration was Methodist's principle of offering equality of pricing. Methodist seeks to negotiate managed care contracts with fair rates and not rely on cost shifting from other customers to maintain the financial integrity of the organization.

As they pursued their strategy, it was becoming clear that a growing managed care presence in their market was having an impact on the kinds of contracts they encountered. This immediate shift made it clear that a dramatic change in performance was required.

Methodist's Chief Executive Officer, David Hitt, recognized the need to address this issue and called together the top 60 leaders of the system for a Saturday retreat to focus on the challenges ahead. During this retreat they were given data that showed the volume challenge they faced and an overview of their customer's expectations. Hitt announced that Methodist would reengineer the processes required to gain a significant increase in performance.

## Governing Structure

During the previous two years the hospital had adopted an approach it refers to as "Value Management." This approach reflects the principles and techniques found in various total quality management programs throughout the country.

The decision to adopt a value management approach included the creation of a value management council. This was made up of the CEO, the CFO, two executive directors, two senior vice presidents, the Vice President of Value Management, Marie Kellam, and two value management coaches. As the events evolved that created the need for a more aggressive approach to improving performance, this group undertook self-education on reengineering, aided by input from their new Director of Reengineering, Mike Phelan. This effort took approximately two months.

The value management council subsequently established a strategic core team (SCT) as the primary governing body over Methodist's reengineering effort. This team was made up of the following 11 staff members:

- Vice President of Information Systems
- Medical Center's Associate Executive Director
- Corporate Finance Accountant
- Hospital Controller
- Director of Admitting
- Director of Reengineering
- Director of Outpatient Services
- Vice President of Value Management
- Director of Security
- Medical Center's Resident Administrator
- Manager of Admitting.

The charter of the SCT included providing the redesign teams with vision, objectives, boundaries, and mission understanding. They offered resource support, helped resolve and prioritize issues, performed cost-benefit analyses on recommendations, and maintained the program schedule throughout the design and implementation phases.

Methodist took seriously the need to gain top management's understanding and support of reengineering. Methodist has a management council that includes approximately 30 leaders in the system. This group was given reading material on reengineering and was asked to submit questions to the Director of Reengineering for further clarification. Then the management council was given presentations to address their questions and gain their support for the reengineering effort.

## Redesign Teams

The SCT created six redesign teams, each focused on an important aspect of outpatient services. These teams were chosen based upon current process orientations before the redesign:

1. Transportation
2. Scheduling
3. Results reporting
4. Patient business operations
5. Diagnostic/treatment services
6. Follow-up and measurements.

Each team was made up of approximately ten people and had a team leader and facilitator. Team leaders and facilitators were responsible for vertical communication among the functions represented on the teams and horizontal communication across the teams. All team leaders were members of the SCT to enable communication of project status and issues across all levels. Facilitators were all drawn from the operational side of the hospital and given team management and work plan training by the Director of Reengineering.

The selection of team members was based on their functional knowledge of the team's process objective and their ability to work within a team. For example, the scheduling team had representatives from the following areas:

- Registration
- Scheduling
- Ambulatory surgery center
- Neuroscience center
- Radiology
- Physiological medicine
- Heart center
- Cancer center.

Each team defined the boundaries of the work within the area they would address, and this "real estate" was subsequently approved by the SCT. This was done to avoid redundant effort and ensure that nothing was being overlooked. The scheduling team addressed these issues:

- Centralized versus decentralized scheduling
- Advance scheduling

- Same-day scheduling
- Physician scheduling
- Receiving/placing orders
- Information systems
- Job consolidation.

The inclusion of information systems input in process redesign occurred in areas where it was determined to be necessary. Specifically, it played a significant role in work of the scheduling team, results reporting team, and patient business operations team.

## Redesign Approach

The redesign teams were trained by the Director of Reengineering and given a charter that sanctioned a broad cross-functional view of outpatient services, the pursuit of an ideal redesign to support the vision and objectives of the reengineering effort, and the obligation to turn implementation plans into reality.

Methodist divided its reengineering effort into two pieces: redesign and implementation. The redesign teams met for four hours each week; two two-hour sessions over a period of four months. The understanding was that the participants would be able to maintain their current positions during this period and still make significant contributions to the redesign effort.

During this time, the teams followed a pragmatic four-step sequential approach:

1. Environmental assessment
2. Current process mapping
3. Ideal process redesign
4. Pre-implementation planning.

During their effort, the teams benchmarked three other hospitals that had either gone through a similar activity or offered useful insights into their outpatient services process. Each team was responsible for creating a final product that consisted of these components:

- Summary of current process from a customer perspective
- Assessment of the impediments Methodist faces in terms of quality of care, cost of care delivery, and quality of worklife
- Recommended redesign, including resource requirements and benefits.

Recall in Chapter 5 the review of redesign options that reengineering teams have considered. One example of how these options helped guide the Methodist Medical Center teams can be seen in a recommendation made in the area of outpatient services. The teams reviewed the circumstances calling for the creation of a caseworker position and benefits that stem from a hybrid centralized/decentralized information access structure.

As they assessed the fragmentation of effort that occurred in the "pre-event" portion of outpatient services, they discovered that the following activities were done by different people in several different clinical service areas:

- Registration
- Scheduling
- Consent forms
- Insurance verification
- Order/entry
- Financial counseling
- Precertification
- Test/treatment rework
- Doctors calling multiple areas for different services.

The cost of all the "hand-offs" was seen in terms of inadequate insurance verification (a minimum verifiable amount of $108,000 per year) and the percent of internal phone calls required to support the exchange of information (52 percent of all phone activity was service area to service area; only 48 percent involved customers). The teams also discovered that the working knowledge of policies and procedures to handle these activities was—at best— fragmented across the organization and often poorly disseminated to people who needed to know the unique requirements of various insurance companies. The ultimate cost of nonquality in this process, however, was a tremendous amount of service area rework and idle time due to incorrect patient information. This caused an unacceptable amount of patient retesting or prevented timely patient arrival in service areas for testing.

*The working knowledge of policies and procedures to handle these activities was—at best—fragmented across the organization.*

The recommended redesign included the creation of a caseworker position that would receive the required training to combine all of the pre-event activities in one point of contact for all physicians and their offices. This included the capability of faxing clinical orders, schedule requests, and patient demographic information to the hospital without picking up a phone. In addition, the team recommended that a redesigned information system support this change by allowing the caseworker to access information required to handle this broad array of responsibilities. The team also recommended that this system be available in satellite areas so that, for example, scheduling patients for follow-up visits could occur without having the patient return to the original point of contact.

The senior sponsors of the reengineering effort reviewed all the team recommendations and made decisions regarding implementation. At this point the work passed to the implementation teams. The separation of redesign from implementation was handled in an interesting manner. Some reengineering experts recommend that those responsible for redesign also be responsible for implementation. They also recommend that the redesign team not return to their previous positions, but inhabit the new environment they create. In the case of Methodist, a middle position was taken.

There were only three implementation teams, but they included several members who had been on the redesign teams. Further, the redesign team members returned to their own areas, but they knew that the implementation of their redesign would alter their own work environment considerably. In short, they *did* have to live with the results.

## Implementation

Methodist is currently undergoing the implementation of the redesign recommendations. They have decided that a first step is a structural reorganization that will allow the outpatient services process to occur in the manner determined by the teams.

Not unlike many other organizations, Methodist found that its outpatient services activity was fragmented across several organizational areas. Its new structure will reflect a realignment of this activity and the changed manner in which it will be performed. They believe this will lead to greater continuity of service, help those involved see themselves as part of a single process, and encourage a team-oriented perspective among those involved.

The implementation faces several organizational issues. Methodist is moving toward a measurement-oriented culture. Each team's redesign included key quality indicators and a description of how they would be measured and reported. The redesigns call for skills-based training, greater emphasis on team-based behavior, and an overall service-based focus throughout the work environment.

## Bottom Line

This organization expects a 22 percent reduction in outpatient-specific labor costs resulting from its reorganization efforts alone. Overall, the Director of Reengineering believes it can achieve a 35 percent improvement because of a greater degree of integration across previously fragmented work activity. They forecast a 30 percent increase in day surgery capacity as a result of their changes. Additional improvements are likely to occur as a result of job consolidation, a change in skills mix among its individual contributors and an increase in the ratio of individual contributors to managers.

## Lessons Learned

The reengineering effort at Methodist has gone quite well. Among the major reasons cited for this are these:

- The selection of teams made up of people who were optimistic, enthusiastic, persistent, and creative problem solvers
- Having a structured workplan that was well managed and allowed no significant deviations
- Exemplary executive support that took the form of public proclamations of intent, dealing effectively with resistance, and standing back to allow the teams the opportunity to do their best work.

Of course, there were things they would try to do better in the future. Team size and composition will be managed more closely, increased emphasis on building trust within cross-functional teams will occur, and the communication of the reengineering effort will have an even higher priority. This will include people directly and indirectly affected by the outcomes.

One might ask, What about the physicians? Since they were not full-time members on the teams, Methodist might have run the risk of losing their support. However, an innovative approach was taken to ensure this did not occur. The office managers for the physicians participated in focus groups to get their input and share with them the progress being made. Further, personal interviews with a large number of physicians were carried out as part of the overall effort. Finally, Methodist's physician advisory group, all ad hoc members of the strategic core team, were briefed every six to eight weeks by the process owner and the Director of Reengineering.

Overall, this is an impressive effort and reflects an appreciation for the mechanics of reengineering and the level of organizational commitment required for success. One cannot help but be impressed by the level of support this effort received from the senior executive level.

# IRVING HEALTHCARE SYSTEM ············

## Background

The Irving Healthcare System is located in Irving, Texas. It has over 250 beds and employs approximately 1,200 people. In 1993 it was recognized in a study done by HCIA/Mercer as one of the top 100 hospitals in the United States. Its president, Michael O'Keefe, FACHE, assumed this position in 1988 and has developed a vision of the organziation over the years that began by emphasizing a theme of delivering the best health care with the best people in the best environment with the best technology. A more modest version was put forward to gain board support in the earlier years: "best mid-sized hospital in north Texas." By 1990, however, he encouraged a broader view, one of being an integrated health care system responsible for the health needs of Irving and the surrounding communities.

## Case for Action

In 1989 Irving had already begun to take steps that resulted in a trend of declining lengths of stay, increased admissions, and ensuring the Medicare portion of their business was kept at 45 percent or lower. However, because of their success, O'Keefe found few people who shared his level of concern over the need to focus on cost. At that time, Irving's monthly bottom line was over $300,000. Today their annual cash flow is over $18 million. This reflects a three-year quality improvement effort that targeted utilization and length of stay. They also moved aggressively to develop critical pathways to address delivery cost while maintaining quality outcomes. One outcome of this effort was the reduction of open-heart surgery stays from ten days to six days and a reduction in overall costs of 20 percent. Irving's CQI effort over these three years saw activity of 90 various teams, some of which focused on service improvements as well as cost and quality. Some achievements included departmental consolidations, work redesign, and staffing changes. The CQI effort has been guided by a quality council of department directors and administrators under the leadership of Jay Macfarland, FACHE, the hospital's COO.

The continued market demand for efficient delivery of high-quality health care led the quality council to conclude that a more aggressive stand was needed to deal with their cost structure. Because 50 percent of their costs were salaries, they decided the best approach to deal with this was a significant redesign of the work performed. They began with a six-week assessment of their operations and used this information to select the processes where redesign was most likely to result in improvement. With the reengineering effort under the direction of the quality council, O'Keefe became deeply involved in alliance discussions with a Dallas health care system, an agreement reached in the latter half of 1994.

The combination of past efforts to redefine Irving's mission, its significant accomplishments through CQI and critical pathways, its new alliance relationship, and its reengineering activity are all aimed at positioning Irving for the changing health care market it faces.

## Governing Structure

The decision to pursue CQI led to the creation of a quality council. The council is made up of administrators and seven department directors representing all areas of the hospital. The council was established to serve as a catalyst in coordinating, supporting, and sustaining process improvement. In this sense, its roles and responsibilities within the current reengineering effort have not changed. But its purpose has moved from focusing predominantly on continuous quality improvement to placing greater emphasis on creating new cross-functional processes that would lead to significantly higher levels of performance. The council's primary duties also include serving as a clearinghouse and forming sub-committees. These committees include communications, quality and finance, and education and human resources.

Irving had identified several strategic objectives that initiated its CQI effort, including the following:

- Gaining greater accountability through a shared decision-making structure
- Improving decision making through improved information access
- Promoting organization interaction through enhanced communication
- Supporting transformation through skills development.

As this list suggests, Irving has had a long history of taking action prior to being in dire straits. The CQI effort drew upon these objectives for guidance. Irving also pursued an investigation of the patient-focused care model. Some of its attributes were similar to reengineering, but Irving concluded that it still resulted in unwanted cost shifting. As they became aware of the need to take stronger action to improve performance, the council investigated several approaches and decided on reengineering. The strategic objectives continue to guide the reengineering activity. In short, the council provides the link between the organization's strategy and the reengineering effort.

To prepare themselves, the council immersed itself in management literature related to reengineering and conducted a Director's retreat that focused on this approach. At that time they brought in individuals from other hospitals who had been successful in this type of activity.

The participants concluded that their past success in CQI and other efforts at change had created an environment that would serve to support reengineering. These experiences included successful decision making in a team-based environment, the consolidation of departments, and the positive results from a cardiovascular project that resulted in significant cost reduction, decreased length of stay, and reduced procedural requirements. The council selected seven processes that would be the initial focus of their effort:

- Acute/critical care, skilled nursing facility
- Physical medicine/rehabilitation
- Surgical services
- Order processing/results/medication distribution
- Transport/messenger services
- Admitting/outpatient registration/discharge
- Home health services.

## Redesign Teams

Seven teams were created to pursue the processes listed above. Approximately ten to twelve people are on each team, plus two external consultants who serve in an advisory capacity. The selection of team members was done by department directors. It should be noted that each team includes a member of the quality council. The teams were to be made up of 60 percent staff and 40 percent supervisors. Each team has a leader, a facilitator, and a mentor.

The team leaders oversee the logistical side of the team's activities, make team assignments and follow up on them, and make presentations to the quality council as requested. The team facilitators oversee the interaction of the team members, helping them keep on track, and encouraging them to "think out of the box." The team mentor acts as a coach and guide, provides support and resources, and helps overcome obstacles. In addition, the mentor reports weekly to the quality council on the team's status.

*The team mentor acts as a coach and guide, provides support and resources, and helps overcome obstacles.*

The teams have a set of objectives that were derived from discussions held by the quality council. For example, the surgical services team is seeking

- Greater coordination of activities between the operating room, day surgery, Patient Acute Care Unit (PACU), nursing units, and ancillary and support services
- To reduce physician and patient waiting time
- To become cost-competitive with freestanding ambulatory surgery centers
- More effective utilization of staff through leveraging of lower-skilled activities to appropriate providers.

This team's members represent the following positions within the hospital:

- RNs from operating room, PACU, day surgery, and medical/surgical unit
- Management representatives from support services and ancillary services
- Surgeon
- Anesthesiologist
- Person knowledgeable in operating room scheduling.

The team members are expected to hold three-hour sessions each week over a five-month period to examine their assigned core process and develop a redesign proposal. This constitutes the design phase of the reengineering effort. To prepare themselves for this work, the teams participated in two presentations developed by the communication subteam of the quality council. The first presented an overview of the market Irving faced and underscored the need for change. The second gave an overview of reengineering. In addition, each team member went through a two-day workshop to provide them specific information on the work they were to do. Team leaders and facilitators are responsible for team orientation insofar as reengineering is concerned. All facilitators received facilitator training as well.

Each of the quality council subcommittees mentioned earlier has a representative on a team. An information services representative is on the following teams: order processing/results/medication distribution and admitting/outpatient registration/discharge. The quality and finance subcommittee is expected to offer each team assistance in areas such as cost-benefit analysis and service enhancement to ensure that the team's redesign outcomes are measurable.

## Redesign Approach

Although the teams do not follow a prescribed set of steps, their "logic path" can be seen by examining the number and purpose of five meetings they hold:

- **Meeting 1** is essentially a "visioning" meeting where the members are oriented to their task, review a workplan, develop a future view of the new process, establish goals and objectives, and identify obstacles and enablers.

- **Meeting 2** focuses more heavily upon the development of new processes that reflect and support the vision. Further work is done on identifying the obstacles and enablers the team needs to consider.

- **Meeting 3** draws upon premeeting work, and the team identifies gaps between the current process and the desired future process. They "map" the processes in terms of key workflow steps and customer contact points. Finally, they develop work measurement tools.

- **Meeting 4** allows the team, to review data collected, compare current performance to best practices, quantify the impact their redesigned process will have on quality, service, and cost, and develop preliminary recommendations that will be presented to the quality council.

- **Meeting 5** focuses on developing implementation plans and finalizing process recommendations. Subsequently, the team presents their recommendations to the quality council.

## Implementation

At this point, Irving has yet to determine the make-up of its implementation teams. They recognize that this will be a critical decision because the types of change they anticipate will mean they need to combine departments and reallocate people to different positions. The inclusion of physicians within the clinically oriented process teams will be essential, but the COO believes that further effort is necessary to ensure support from this group.

## Lessons Learned

As Irving's redesign teams begin their work, a number of lessons have already become apparent:

- They need to ensure that the role of external consultant is made clear. Irving had less need for facilitating than

for a proactive contribution (e.g., benchmarking information).

- The past CQI experience has proved very helpful. Not only
are people more comfortable working in a team-based
environment, they are aware of how problem solving
should be done as a team. Concerns over the need for
change were dealt with earlier among some who resisted
it.

- Reengineering is becoming understood to be as much
of an emotional exercise as a mechanical one. Many
people still are concerned that it is only another name
for downsizing. Some feel this may dampen the creativity
needed on the teams. Irving believes it needs to do more
in the way of communication and education to help deal
with this.

## Bottom Line

The Irving Healthcare System is a good example of an organization
that is somewhere between "seeing trouble" and "causing trouble."
Instead of waiting until they were "in trouble," they have taken
several significant steps—even prior to reengineering—to help
position themselves for the highly competitive health care market
they face.

It is hard not to be impressed with the ability of an organization of this size to take such a view and then move forward in
this manner. Although their reengineering effort has just begun,
they have already benefited from their past change efforts and
have strong leadership support for reengineering and a climate
that many people believe will encourage creative redesign options.

## ·········· A HEALTH CARE INSURER

### Background

Although hospitals are clearly pursuing reengineering, so are
others in our industry, including the major health care insurer
highlighted here. This organization, despite having a well-designed
reengineering effort, has been quite "shy" in touting its progress.
I am hopeful the readers will bear with me as I offer an overview
of this effort, while taking care to respect the organization's desire
for anonymity.

### Case for Action

This insurer has identified several key external forces that will
require them to make dramatic changes in how they go to market

and in the internal processes to make this possible. As with other insurers, this organization is a highly visible portion of the health care cost equation and is a target for government and public scrutiny.

More specifically, this business is concerned it could lose its historic leverage with provider networks. This would result from consolidations of provider organizations so they can share risk, reduce operating costs, and offer a broader base of service. Customers are also looking for evidence that insurers are taking steps to address the rising costs of health care. Successful insurers of the future must introduce innovative managed care products that allow subscribers desired flexibility in choosing health care, combined with arrangements with providers that eliminate cost-inflating practices such as fragmented billing.

Clearly, moving from a traditional indemnity mindset to one that focuses on managed care is the only way for this business to survive in the future. But doing so means being able to do the following:

- Build strong provider relationships and networks that emphasize credentialing and qualifying providers, measuring quality of care, and analysis of treatment outcomes
- Insulate the customer from administrative details, with all payment and treatment administration handled directly between providers and the insurer
- Offer a wide range of contractual arrangements with a variety of networks
- Increase emphasis on support of preventive care services and treatment plans
- Improve provider incentives to deliver cost-effective and high-quality medical care
- Ensure development and deployment of "tailor made" products (e.g. selling networks; hybrid fully underwritten products; managed care programs; and selling/marketing information).

Several warning signs already exist to suggest that time is running out for this business if it does not move swiftly to strengthen its competitive position. It is witnessing rising administrative costs and having difficulty administering one of its new products, and it has been unable to meet performance requirements of one of its past customers. An internal survey of its employees found that a sizable percentage did not believe the organization was working efficiently. Unfortunately, historic patterns of activity to address efficiency included adding more management positions and layers, more staff positions, and more auditing functions, and attempting fragmented fixes to unit or divisional problems. All resulted in a continued increase in administrative costs with little effect on overall organizational efficiency.

The senior executives of this organization, through their strategic planning process, identified critical areas that needed to change to enable them to thrive in a managed care market. From this came a decision to use reengineering to address two key processes as a first step in a major organizational redirection.

## Governing Structure

This organization formed a steering committee that includes the CEO and several senior-level executives whose roles and responsibilities closely resemble the structure we discussed in Chapter 4. In addition, a senior vice president serves as an "executive sponsor" to champion the reengineering effort. A "coordinating group" consists of senior managers who have responsibility for obtaining resources for the effort, maintaining communication, and resolving issues. An office of reengineering is the equivalent of a "czar" but involves a small group instead of a single individual. Core process owners were selected, as were core process teams.

It is interesting how this structure reflects the overall culture. This organization has a long bureaucratic history. Its multiple layers and management, strict adherence to functional boundaries, and overlapping committees have often resulted in severely delayed decisions. These include setting organizational direction and changing internal processes. Although this governing structure accurately reflects—and has attempted to address—this historical working environment, it runs the risk of mirroring the status quo.

This governing structure currently oversees two core processes and supporting business processes, that were identified as being most critical to redirecting the organization:

**Core Process:** Group and Member Acquisition

**Business Processes:**

- *Market and sales analysis*: the activities required to develop target markets, through an understanding of market and competitive environmental factors.
- *Advertising and promotion*: the activities required to influence the marketplace to bring about positive action in our target markets.

- *Distribution*: the activities required to establish contact with our target markets and create potential customers.
- *Group and member set-up*: the activities required to transition potential customers to enrolled customers.

**Core Process:** Medical Services Performance

**Business Processes:**

- *Wellness management*: the identification of the patient's health status and the management of disease risk.
- *Illness management*: the segmentation and management of patient conditions through a life cycle of illness that may be acute, chronic, catastrophic, or terminal in nature.
- *Relationship management*: the collection, processing, analysis, and sharing of health information to facilitate delivery system performance improvement and optimal health outcomes for our customers.
- *Medical services information integration*: the management of relationships with providers through education, communication, and information designed to achieve shared performance goals and meet member and provider expectations.

## Redesign Teams

Each of the teams consists of approximately a dozen members. They were chosen based on their past experiences in areas affected by the reengineering effort or their expertise in areas that would support the team's activity. Some, for example, were involved in the development of the reengineering methodology and tools, some come from information systems positions, and others are from positions where knowledge of the business processes was critical.

*Each person is expected to participate on the team on a full-time basis for approximately nine months to a year.*

Each team has a facilitator whose job is to help in coaching the team, documenting the work performed, helping the team deal with the diversity of participants, and ensuring the team adheres to agreed-upon behavioral norms. One particularly interesting aspect of the team's assignments is the intensity and length of their involvement. Each person is expected to participate on the team on a full-time basis for approximately nine months to a year.

## Redesign Approach

The overall approach used by the teams reflects the models described in Chapter 4. Their equivalent of a business reengineering model has these components:

- Executive direction setting
- Establish business transformation infrastructure
- Mobilize core process teams
- Reengineer core processes design
- Realign corporate infrastructure
- Develop systems capabilities
- Develop corporate transition plan
- Develop and implement continuous improvement process
- Implement reengineered core processes and capabilities.

Bounding this activity are two other components. One focuses on communication, education, and training. The other involves managing the overall business transformation effort.

The team activity follows a four-step model: planning, current assessment, process reengineerng, and implementation. The actual work closely parallels process reengineering.

## Implementation

It will be several months before this organization will begin to implement their redesigned processes. At the time of this writing, each team had completed the planning step and had received approval from senior executives to pursue the current assessment step.

## Lessons Learned

One of the more interesting aspects of this particular case is the sequence of events leading up to the decision to pursue reengineering. As it turns out, the organization had decided some time earlier that it needed a far more efficient means of processing insurance claims. The original solution was to develop information technology capability to do just that.

As this "solution" moved forward, it became clear to some that the organization needed much more than a new claims system. A senior executive took over this effort and concluded that a much broader scope of change was required. What happened from that point forward is an example of putting the technology cart before the reengineering horse. In short, a large consulting firm was brought in to help develop a vision of where the organization needed to be and then assist in the creation of an approach to get there. The approach required a small army of consultants whose primary focus was the development of information technology solutions in support of the vision.

There were two issues, however, that served to undermine this effort. First, the technology solution lacked a broad base of organizational sanction—the technology consultants had little contact with those whose work would ultimately be affected by this change. A more important issue, however, was that the overall vision guiding the effort was never tied into an organizational strategy developed, debated, and agreed to by the senior executives.

As the call for health care reform grew louder and the price for a delayed response became more apparent, the decision was made to reverse the "cart" and the "horse." The organization publicly acknowledged the reengineering effort that had been designed and developed somewhat quietly for over a year. That effort resulted in methodology, tools, and training to guide the work of process teams.

Several senior executive planning sessions were held to gain consensus on the organization's direction and, subsequently, understanding and support required to pursue the reengineering of selected core processes. This led to the effort described above.

What are the key lessons here? One need only review the principles of reengineering to see that the organization should have begun with a strategic repositioning vision—developed by the executive team—that would drive the reengineering effort. This would have shortened the time frame to begin reengineering. Equally important, it would have offered the senior executives an opportunity to learn more about this approach to ensure that they knew what the implications would be in the future. Finally, leading with a technology solution before beginning a process redesign effort runs counter to reengineering principles. Technology should "enable" change, not drive it.

As this organization moves forward, it has several points in its favor. The methodology is sound, the tools used by the teams are helping their effort, and the selection of process owners and team members has ensured that considerable talent has been assembled and focused on serious business processes. Senior management has also given a strong endorsement for reengineering and its expectations for performance improvement.

At the present time, there still are those in the organization who are not convinced that this approach is necessary or will result in the performance gains being sought. Clearly, this will require sustained effort at communication and education—something that nearly every reengineering effort elsewhere has also found to be the case.

## Bottom Line

This organization has no choice but to pursue a rigorous reengineering effort. It has—somewhat belatedly—moved aggressively to do so. As time has progressed, it has come to accept the fact that reengineering principles are more than just words on paper. Violating them is not only costly, it can result in a significant loss of business opportunity.

The true test of this organization's reengineering effort will come within the next few months when it attempts to implement the redesigned processes described earlier. Given the history of the organization and the way in which change has been addressed in the past, this is going to be a major challenge. Personally, I believe this example should be regarded as closer to the norm for reengineering efforts. That they are where they are today is testimony to their ability to adapt and redirect themselves in the face of a changing market. This alone makes them worthy of our consideration—and emulation.

## CONCLUSION

It is clear from these examples that the organizations have "done it right." These organizations represent the "second wave" of reengineering in health care. The first wave often suffered from most, if not all, of the causes for failure discussed earlier. In these cases, however, a fair bit of planning and education preceded the commitment to move forward. Perhaps the most impressive aspects of these cases is the degree to which health care reengineering has been linked to each organization's strategy, and the high degree of commitment given to the effort by senior management.

Although each of these organizations would admit they have far to go, the groundwork has been laid carefully and they continue to learn from their successes and mistakes. They serve as models of what hospitals and other health care organizations will have to do to take advantage of the power of health care reengineering.

# Epilogue

**S**OME YEARS ago I listened to a presentation by Richard Walton, a Harvard professor. Among other work, he authored a seminal article calling for a movement from a control-oriented work environment to one that encourages people to make a deeper commitment to an organization. Ironically he was offering this perspective to an audience at GE, one that would be decimated within 12 months from massive layoffs and restructuring. After he spoke, I approached him with this reaction: Calling for such a shift in thinking assumes that it can occur through rational appeals. From what I had observed, this is not a safe bet.

Over the past year I was reminded of that observation as I saw how the various factions within the health care reform debate framed up their arguments. Emotionally charged rhetoric obscured what few facts were available. Seeking to protect their positions from change, various interest groups combined half-truths with shameless efforts to create fear and distrust among their audiences. Those who benefit from and therefore support the status quo won the ultimate victory: paralysis.

*Those who benefit from and therefore support the status quo won the ultimate victory: paralysis.*

Afterward, even those who had participated in this activity seemed a bit chagrined at the outcome. A few began to call anew for a more "sensible" set of options to be considered at a later date. But we had just witnessed the triumph of emotion over rationality. What makes anyone think that, flush with such an achievement, the protectors of "business as usual" would be reluctant to offer a second rendition if necessary? Someone once said that if you are receiving flak, you are probably over the target. This is true for reengineering as well as health care reform. In both instances, calls for a radical shift in direction have brought forth criticism that this choice of direction is overkill, and that the circumstances don't warrant such dramatic efforts.

The history of attempts to achieve performance improvement demonstrate that "quick fixes" fail to attack the essence of the problem. As Peter Drucker has said, when the theory of business is wrong, only a shift in theory and a redesign of core processes to support it will achieve the needed change. His perspective is as true for health care as for any other industry. We have only postponed the inevitable. Meanwhile, reality will continue the pressure for change through global capitation and the increasing number of uninsured people, among other factors. Anyone who thinks this is not leading to upheaval is mistaken. Anyone who thinks it is possible to "continuously improve" themselves out of this predicament is also mistaken. Calls for a hiatus in the discussion of health care reform reflect an emotional state—not one based on rationality. Likewise, criticisms of reengineering as an approach for change ignore the unshakable principles that support it.

## ANOTHER ONE BITES THE DUST?

What if there was a national consensus that reengineering was just another fad? Well, it wouldn't matter. The fact is that the history behind reengineering is quite long and draws upon the knowledge and experience gained across several disciplines. The issues never go away. As Aldus Huxley once said, "Facts do not cease to exist because they are ignored." One can dismiss reengineering—or any other approach, for that matter—and this only brings us back to the same point: How can a health care organization achieve a significant improvement in performance?

We have already learned that nibbling around the periphery doesn't get it. Even if the label "reengineering" loses its cachet over time, its underlying premise will certainly resurface and be absorbed within another approach. This is an example of "pay me now or pay me later."

## THE LAND OF TURBO-BUBBA

Politicians who blame the genetically flawed electorate for the problems in the country remind me of the leaders of organizations who complain about their miserable workforce. One of the more appealing attributes of reengineering is that it calls people on their myopia.

Personally, I like who we are. The vast majority of people I have worked with over the years demonstrate a very sensible form of survival. They size up the environment and do what is necessary to survive in it—or leave. The people who will change the health care industry—for the most part—are those who are already working within it. If you want them to do this, however, it will be necessary to change the conditions that surround them, including work processes and the infrastructure that supports them.

It is pointless to complain that the current workforce is not made up of brilliant individuals. Few are. It is not worth trying to pursue brilliance. What *is* worth our effort is the redesign of organizations so we "bubbas" (my term for a person who is limited to a degree) can—at the very least—become "turbo-bubbas" by having access to information and the opportunity to strut our stuff within a less cumbersome set of processes. This is not a humanitarian issue—it is the way to beat the pants off competitors who simply can't figure out how to tap into the mother lode—people.

## SO NOW WE KNOW

As we conclude our conversation it is worth looking back and identifying ten key conclusions from these cases and the material presented in this book:

1. Given the magnitude of change in health care, and the time frame within which to address it, health care reengineering is a reasonable choice of approaches.

2. Reengineering requires a senior team to set the stage for it, tie it directly to the organization's strategy, and stand ready to support it. Anything less will result in yet another lost opportunity for significant improvement.

3. A comparison of reengineering to other approaches concludes that it can be differentiated on several criteria. It is the most aggressive of those considered and, given the turmoil it will create, should not be chosen on a whim. But there is no doubt that it is *different* from the others and should not be dismissed without serious consideration.

4. It is impossible to ignore the dramatic performance improvements that are being attributed to reengineering. The health care organizations that are getting behind this are reaping enormous value. Claims that "no one exactly like us has done it" simply create a smokescreen to obscure some rather unattractive motives for avoiding serious change.

5. Health care reengineering must go beyond mere process redesign. An organization needs to wrap itself around this effort and ensure that it receives support and guidance as it

moves forward. The realignment of infrastructure will be a critical issue in determining success. Unwillingness to do this will subvert the redesign potential.

*An organization needs to wrap itself around this effort and ensure that it receives support and guidance as it moves forward.*

6. The teams of people who are asked to reengineer health care processes face an enormous job. They need training and tools and a "road map" to help them. The choice of members, their level of commitment, and the degree of freedom they receive to do their work will be the limiting factors in redesign.

7. The mystery surrounding health care processes is greatly exaggerated. Further, the range of redesign options is far less intimidating than some have thought. They are knowable and health care applications that fit them are becoming clear.

8. The degree of political commitment required to increase the probability of success has been articulated clearly. Choosing to reengineer without providing this level of support is a deathwish.

9. Any further reengineering failures cannot be attributed to ignorance of the causes. The track record of several companies who have stumbled is open for review and the list of "potholes" is more than sufficient to avoid disaster.

10. Health care reengineering is a form of large-scale organization change. Understanding how to embed change principles within such an effort is critical to ensuring that change can be implemented without experiencing "total melt down."

## THE ROAD AHEAD

We come to the end of our conversation about how health care reengineering can bring about dramatic change. The points raised and suggestions made in this book are worth considering for those who become involved in such efforts. For those who are on the fence, you now have a better sense of what this will involve and can make your decisions accordingly.

The "change riders" who accept this challenge will find that confronting the status quo is the hardest thing they will ever do. The most successful people I know are those who maintain their integrity in the face of fierce resistance. I admire them immensely because they have decided not to spend the rest of their careers staring at the underside of mediocrity. I leave you with these words of advice: Just because you are outnumbered doesn't mean you are wrong.

# Bibliography

Abramowitz, K. S. 1993. *The Future of Healthcare Delivery in America*. New York: Sanford C. Bernstein Company.

Adams, S. 1989. *Always Postpone Meetings with Time-Wasting Morons*. New York: Topper Books.

———. 1991. *Build a Better Life by Stealing Office Supplies*. New York: Topper Books.

Anders, G. 1994. "In Age of the HMO, Pioneer of the Species Has Hit a Rough Patch." *The Wall Street Journal*, 1 December.

Anders, G., and H. Stout. 1994. "With Congress Stalled, Health Care Is Shaped by the Private Sector." *The Wall Street Journal*, 26 August.

Arnett, G. M. 1994. "It's Taxation, Stupid." *The Wall Street Journal*, 29 March.

Arnoudse, D., V. DiBianca, and M. Milleman. 1994. "Executive Team Alignment: The Unifying Force in Reengineering." *Insights Quarterly* (Spring): 50–61.

Azevedo, D. 1995. "Can the World's Largest Integrated Health System Learn to Feel Small?" *Medical Economics* (23 January): 82–101.

Bardwick, J. 1991. *Danger in the Comfort Zone*. New York: AMACOM.

Beer, M., B. Spector, P. R. Lawrence, D. Quinn Mills, and R. E. Walton. 1984. *Managing Human Assets*. New York: The Free Press.

Beer, M., R. A. Eisenstat, and B. Spector. 1990. "Why Change Programs Don't Produce Change." *Harvard Business Review* 68 (November–December): 158–65.

Benjamin, R. I., and E. Levinson. 1993. "A Framework for

Managing IT-Enabled Change." *Sloan Management Review* (Summer): 23–33.

Bennis, W. 1989 *Why Leaders Can't Lead.* San Francisco: Jossey-Bass.

Bennis, W., and B. Nanus. 1985. *Leaders.* New York: Harper & Row.

Bergman, R. 1994. "Reengineering Health Care." *Hospitals & Health Networks* 68 (5 February): 28–36.

Boland, P., ed. 1993. *Making Managed Healthcare Work.* Gaithersburg, MD: Aspen Publishers.

Boss, R. W. 1989. *Organization Development in Health Care.* Reading, MA: Addison-Wesley.

Brown, T. 1994. "Deengineering the Corporation." *Industry Week* 243 (18 April): 18–26.

Bulkeley, W. M. 1994. "The Latest Big Thing at Many Companies Is Speed, Speed, Speed." *The Wall Street Journal,* 23 December.

Byrne, J. A. 1993. "The Horizontal Corporation." *Business Week* (20 December): 76–81.

Caldwell, B. 1994. "Missteps, Miscues." *Information Week* (20 June): 38–44.

Cascio, W. F. 1993. "Downsizing: What Do We Know? What Have We Learned?" *Academy of Management Executive* 7 (1): 95–104.

Champy, J. 1995. *Reengineering Management.* New York: Harper Business.

Cherns, A. 1976. "The Principles of Sociotechnical Design." *Human Relations* (29): 783–92.

Ciampa, D. 1992. *Total Quality: A User's Guide for Implementation.* Reading, MA: Addison-Wesley.

Conlin, R. B. 1993. "Are Malpractice Awards the Demon of Health Care?" *USA Today,* 5 May.

Copple, R. C. 1993. "Patient Care Redesign Process, Budget Neutrality, Analysis, and Results." *1993 HIMSS Conference Proceedings* (3): 243–54.

Davenport, T. H. 1993. *Process Innovation.* Boston: Harvard Business School Press.

Davenport, T. H., and J. E. Short. 1990. "The New Industrial Engineering Information Technology and Business Process Redesign." *Sloan Management Review* (Summer): 11–26.

Drucker, P. F. 1994. "The Theory of the Business." *Harvard Business Review* (September–October): 95–104.

Dunbar, C. 1994. "MultiCare Health System Saves Millions of Dollars through Redesigned Care." *Health Management Technology* 15 (July): 22–29.

Eskow, R. H. 1993. "Collection, Correction, Application: The Information Cycle in Managed Healthcare." In *Making Managed Healthcare Work*, edited by P. Boland, 445–78. Gaithersburg, MD: Aspen Publishers.

Farney, E. 1994. "Have Liberals Ignored 'Have-Less' Whites at Their Own Peril?" *The Wall Street Journal*, 14 December.

Fischer, R., and R. Canion. 1992–1993. "Beyond Re-engineering, Beyond Outsourcing: Business Integration—The Next Natural Step." *Professional Review* (Winter): 18–20.

Fried, L. 1991. "A Blueprint for Change." *Computerworld*, 2 December. 91–95.

Friedman, M. 1993. "The Folly of Buying Health Care at the Company Store." *The Wall Street Journal*, 3 February.

Furey, T. R. 1993. "A Six-Step Guide to Process Reengineering." *Planning Review* 21, (March–April): 20–23.

Gabor, A. 1990. *The Man Who Discovered Quality*. New York: Random House.

Galbraith, J. R. 1994. *Competing with Flexible Lateral Organizations*. Reading, MA: Addison-Wesley.

Garvin, D. A. 1993. "Building a Learning Organization." *Harvard Business Review* 71 (July–August): 78–91.

Gaucher, E. J., and R. J. Coffey. 1993. *Total Quality in Healthcare*. San Francisco, Jossey-Bass.

Goodstein, L. D., and W. W. Burke. 1991. "Creating Successful Organization Change." *Organization Dynamics* 19 (4): 5–13.

Graulich, D. 1993. "Reengineering Efficiency into a Blue Cross Organization." *Insights Quarterly* (Fall): 64–69.

Greene, J. 1995. "Merger Monopolies." *Modern Healthcare*, 5 December, 38–48.

Greenwood, T., A. Wasson, and R. Giles. 1993. "The Learning Organization: Concepts, Processes, and Questions." *Performance & Instruction* (April): 7–11.

Griffith, J. R., V. K. Sahney, and R. A. Mohr. 1995. *Reengineering Health Care: Building on CQI*. Ann Arbor, MI: Health Administration Press.

Gulden, G. K., and R. H. Reck. 1992. "Combining Quality and Reengineering Efforts for Process Excellence." *Information Strategy: The Executive's Journal* 8 (Spring): 10–16.

Halal, W. E. 1994. "From Hierarchy to Enterprise: Internal Markets Are the New Foundation of Management." *The Academy of Management Executive*. 8 (November): 69–83.

Hall, G., J. Rosenthal, and J. Wade. 1993. "How to Make Reengineering *Really* Work." *Harvard Business Review* 71 (November–December): 119–31.

Hamel, G., and C. K. Prahalad. 1994. "Competing for the Future." *Harvard Business Review*, 68 (July–August): 122–28.

Hammer, M., and J. Champy. 1993. *Reengineering the Corporation.* New York: Harper Business.

Hammer, M., and S. A. Stanton. 1995. *The Reengineering Revolution.* New York: Harper Business.

Hammonds, K. H., K. Kevin, and K. Thurston. 1994. "The New World of Work." *Business Week*, (17 October): 76–87.

Harrar, G. 1994. "Talking Reality." *Enterprise* (January): 20–23.

Harrison, B. D. 1993. "A Methodology for Reengineering Businesses." *Planning Review* 21 (March–April): 6–11.

Helppie, R. D. 1992. "A Time for Reengineering." *Computers in Healthcare* 13 (January): 22–24.

Hill, C., and Y. Ken. 1992. "Staying Power: Motorola Illustrates How an Aged Giant Can Remain Vibrant." *The Wall Street Journal*, 9 December.

Johansson, H. J., P. McHugh, A. J. Pendlebury, and W. A. Wheeler III. 1993. *Business Process Reengineering.* New York: John Wiley.

Jordan, P. 1993. "Testing Simulations Offer a Low-Cost, No-Risk Preview." *Enterprise* (July): 36–40.

Keidel, R. W. 1994. "Rethinking Organizational Design." *The Academy of Management Executive* 8, (4): 12–31.

Kertesz, L. 1994. "California Nurses File Suit to Stop Work Redesign," *Modern Healthcare* (19 September): 14.

———. 1995. "California System Sees Results from Radical Restructuring." *Modern Healthcare* (24 April): 32–33.

Kilmann, R. H. 1988. *Beyond the Quick Fix: Managing Five Tracks to Organizational Success.* San Francisco: Jossey-Bass.

King, J. 1994. "Re-engineering Slammed." *Computerworld* 28 (13 June): 1, 14.

Kissler, G. D. 1991. *The Change Riders.* Reading, MA: Addison-Wesley.

———. 1994. "The New Employment Contract." *Human Resource Management* 33 (3): 335–52.

———. 1995. "Reengineering Patient Account Management." *Journal of Patient Account Management* (January): 12–15.

Klein, M. M. 1994. "The Most Fatal Reengineering Mistakes." *Information Strategy* (Summer): 21–28.

Kongstvedt, P. R., ed. 1993. *The Managed Health Care Handbook.* Gaithersburg, MD: Aspen Publishers.

Lado, A. A., and M. C. Wilson. 1994. "Human Resource Systems and Sustained Competitive Advantage: A Competency-Based Perspective." *Academy of Management Review* 19 (October): 699–727.

Lawler, E. E., III. 1988. *High-Involvement Management.* San Francisco: Jossey-Bass.

Lawler, E. E., III. 1994. "Total Quality Management and Employee Involvement: Are They Compatible?" *Academy of Management Executive* 8 (1): 68–76.

Lipin, S. 1993. "A New Vision: Citicorp Chief Reed, Once a Big Thinker, Gets Down to Basics." *The Wall Street Journal,* 25 May.

Lowenthal, J. N. 1994. *Reengineering the Organization: A Step-by-Step Approach to Corporate Revitalization.* Milwaukee, WI: ASQC Quality Press.

Luke, R., and R. W. Boss. 1981. "Barriers Limiting the Implementation of Quality Assurance Programs." *Health Services Research* 16: 305–14.

Majchrzak, A. 1988. *The Human Side of Factory Automation.* San Francisco: Jossey-Bass Publishers.

Mandel, M. J. 1994. "Business Rolls the Dice." *Business Week,* (17 October): 88–90.

Mankin, D., T. Bikson, B. Gutek, and C. Stasz. 1988. "Managing Technological Change: The Process Is Key." *Datamation* (15 September): 69–80.

Mayo, E. 1977. *The Human Problems of Industrial Civilization.* New York: Arno Press.

Meyer, C. 1994. "How the Right Measures Help Teams Excel." *Harvard Business Review* 72 (May–June): 95–103.

Moad, J. 1994. "Reengineering: Report from the Trenches." *Datamation* (15 March): 36–40.

Moore, N., and H. Komras. 1993. *Patient-Focused Healing.* San Francisco: Jossey-Bass.

Morris, D., and J. Brandon. 1992. "Reengineering: More than Meets the Eye." *Computers in Healthcare* 13 (November): 52–54.

Nipper, W. D., and E. Farmer. 1993. "Patient-Focused Hospital: Implementation Results." *1993 HIMSS Conference Proceedings* (2): 26–33.

Noble, D. F. 1986. *Forces of Production: A Social History of Industrial Automation.* New York: Oxford University Press.

Ostroff, F., and D. Smith. 1992. "Redesigning the Corporation: The Horizontal Organization." New York: McKinsey & Company. 11–27.

Overman, S. 1994. "Reengineering, TQM Team for Results." *Society for Human Resource Management/HR News* (May): 1, 4.

Palmer, G. M., and S. G. Burns. 1993. "Revolutionizing the Business: Strategies for Succeeding with Change." *Human Resource Planning* 15, (1): 77–84.

Pasmore, W. A. 1988. *Designing Effective Organizations: The Sociotechnical Systems Approach.* New York: John Wiley & Sons.

Pasmore, W., and J. Scherwood. 1978. *Sociotechnical Systems: A Sourcebook.* San Diego, CA: University Associates.

Pearce, J. A., II, and F. Davis. 1987. "Corporate Mission Statements: The Bottom Line." *Academy of Management Executive* (May): 109–16.

Prahalad, C. K., and G. Hamel. 1990. "The Competence of the Corporation." *Harvard Business Review* 68 (May–June): 79–91.

Rai, A., and D. Paper. 1994. "Successful Reengineering through IT Investment." *Information Strategy* (Summer): 18–23.

Reger, R. K., J. V. Mullane, L. T. Gustafson, and S. M. DeMarie. 1994. "Creating Earthquakes to Change Organizational Mindsets." *The Academy of Management Executive* 8 (November): 31–47.

Rifkin, G. 1993. "Reengineering Aetna." *Forbes ASAP* (7 June): 78–86.

Rigby, D. 1993. "The Secret History of Process Reengineering." *Planning Review* (March–April): 24–26.

Roberts, D., R. Kremsdorf, J. Tomabeni, and A. K. Tinker. 1993. "Clinical Decision Support at the Bedside: The New Patient-Centered Hospital." *1993 HIMSS Conference Proceedings* (3): 140–51.

Rosen, J. I., and S. A. Stanton. 1993. "The Rapid Approach to Reengineering." *Insights Quarterly* (Fall): 26–39.

Rummler, G. A., and A. P. Brache. 1990. *Improving Performance.* San Francisco, Jossey-Bass.

Sashkin, M., and J. K. Kenneth. 1993. *Putting Total Quality Management to Work.* San Francisco: Berrett-Koehler.

Sassen, J. A., R. Neff, S. Hattangadi, and S. Sansoni. 1994. "The Winds of Change Blow Everywhere." *Business Week,* (17 October): 92–93.

Schaffer, R. H., and H. A. Thomson. 1992. "Successful Change Programs Begin with Results." *Harvard Business Review* 70 (January–February): 80–89.

Schartner, C. 1993. "Principles of Patient-Focused Care." *Healthcare Information Management* 7 (Spring): 11–15.

Schoemaker, P. J. H. 1992. "How to Link Strategic Vision to Core Capabilities." *Sloan Management Review* (Fall): 67–81.

Schrage, M. 1994. "How to Take the Organizational Temperature." *The Wall Street Journal,* 7 November.

Scites, J. L. 1993. "Transforming the Dinosaur." *Best's Review* (November): 76, 77, 122.

Senge, P. M. 1990. *The Fifth Discipline.* New York: Doubleday.

Shortell, S. M. 1988. "The Evolution of Hospital Systems: Unfulfilled Promises and Self-Fulfilling Prophecies." *Medical Care Review* 45 (20): 177–214.

Shortell, S. M., E. M. Morrison, and B. Friedman. 1992. *Strategic Choices for America's Hospitals.* San Francisco: Jossey-Bass.

Shriver, K. 1994. "Study: Most Hospitals Will Try Integration Despite Obstacles." *Modern Healthcare,* (12 December): 4.

Slavin, L., and B. McWilliams. 1994. "Design for a New Beginning." *Enterprise* (January): 15–17.

Stalk, G., Jr. 1993. "Japan's Dark Side of Time." *Harvard Business Review* 71 (July–August): 93–102.

Stalk, G., Jr., P. Evans, and L. E. Shulman. 1992. "Competing on Capabilities: The New Rules of Corporate Strategy." *Harvard Business Review* 70 (March–April): 57–69.

Stalk, G., Jr., and T. M. Hout. 1990. *Competing against Time.* New York: The Free Press.

Stanton, S., M. Hammer, and B. Power. 1992. "From Resistance to Results: Mastering the Organizational Issues of Reengineering." *Insights Quarterly* (Fall): 6–15.

Stelzer, I. M. 1994. "There Is No Health Care Crisis." *The Wall Street Journal,* 25 January.

Stewart, T. A. 1993. "Reengineering: The Hot New Managing Tool." *Fortune,* (23 August): 41–48.

Strassman, P. A. 1994. "The Hocus-Pocus of Reengineering." *Across the Board* 31 (June): 35–38.

Teisberg, E., O. Olmsted, M. E. Porter, and G. B. Brown. 1994. "Making Competition in Health Care Work." *Harvard Business Review* 72 (July–August): 131–41.

Thomas, P. R. 1990. *Competitiveness through Total Cycle Time.* New York: McGraw-Hill.

———. 1991. *Getting Competitive,* New York: McGraw-Hill.

Thurow, L. 1992. *Head on Head.* New York: William Morrow and Company.

Tichy, N. 1993. "Revolutionize Your Company." *Fortune* (13 December): 114–18.

Tichy, N. and M. Devanna. 1986. *The Transformational Leader.* New York: John Wiley & Sons.

Toffler, A. 1990. *PowerShift.* New York: Bantam Books.

———. 1980. *The Third Wave.* New York: Telecom Library.

Tomsho, R. 1994. "Mounting Sense of Job Malaise Prompts More Health-Care Workers to Join Unions." *The Wall Street Journal,* 9 June.

Trist, E., and K. Bamforth. 1951. "Some Social and Psychological Consequences of the Longwall Method of Coal-Getting." *Human Relations* (1): 3–38.

Troup, N. C. 1992. "World Class Healthcare™ Revolutionizing the Way Hospitals Do Business." *Healthcare Information Management* 6 (Winter): 3–38.

Tufo, H. M., and H. E. Davis. 1993. "Quality Control in the Delivery of Healthcare in the State of Vermont." In *Making Managed Healthcare Work*, edited by P. Boland, 433–37. Gaithersburg, MD: Aspen Publishers.

Ulrich, D., and D. Lake. 1990. *Organizational Capability.* New York: John Wiley & Sons.

Valente, J. 1994. "British Airways Sees Strong Gains, Challenges Ahead." *The Wall Street Journal,* 8 November.

Wachel, W. 1994. "Reengineering: Beyond Incremental Change." *Healthcare Executive* 9 (July–August): 18–21.

Waldholz, M. 1993. "Drug Makers' Image Ills Are Self-Induced." *The Wall Street Journal,* 30 March.

Walton, M. 1986. *The Deming Management Method.* New York: Dodd Mead & Co.

Walton, R. E. 1985. "From Control to Commitment in the Workplace." *Harvard Business Review* 63 (March–April): 77–84.

Winslow, R., and G. Anders. 1993. "Medical Industry Scrambles to Keep Up with Changes." *The Wall Street Journal,* 13 September.

Wolper, L. F. (ed.) 1995. *Health Care Administration,* 2d ed. Gaithersburg, MD: Aspen Publishers.

Woolfe, R. 1992. "The Path to Strategic Alignment." *Indications* 9 (2): 1–13.

Zimmerman, D., and J. J. Skalko. 1994. *Reengineering Health Care.* Franklin, WI: Eagle Press.

Zuboff, S. 1988. *In the Age of the Smart Machine.* New York: Basic Books.

# Index

# About the Author

GARY D. KISSLER is the president of Performance Innovation, Inc., a Dallas-based health care reengineering organization. This business offers workshops in health care reengineering and consulting support for organizations involved in reengineering efforts. Dr. Kissler received a Ph.D. in industrial/organizational psychology from the University of Tennessee.

He has 20 years of domestic and international experience in change management, human resources management, and process reengineering in the manufacturing and service sectors. He has delivered innovative solutions to a wide variety of complex business problems. His publications include several articles and a previous book, *The Change Riders: Managing the Power of Change* (Addison-Wesley, 1991).